"*Hour of The Wolf* is one of the v[...] ac-cessible books I have ever read on [...] time and the ability we have been given to be the artists of own lives. Read this book if you want to fearlessly face the awe-inspiring truth that you can be the hero of your own life! Read this book if you want to live every day with more meaning, purpose, compassion, vitality, and love. Be prepared to never again be asleep while awake and to have many a good night sleep. Paul Lipton is a storyteller and wisdom teacher extraordinaire, and his book is one of amazing grace. You will finish *Hour of the Wolf*, take a deep breath, say thank you, and never live the same way again."

> —**Rabbi Irwin Kula,** author of *Yearnings: Embracing the Sacred Messiness of Life*

"*Hour of the Wolf* riveted our attention from the very beginning. Though his life story is unique—as are all of ours—Paul unerringly and bravely pulls out of his magic hat of life experience just what it is that we can see, and must not look away from, if we are to live our lives with a full measure of wholehearted presence, awareness, wonderment, and yes, even joy. Authentic and compassionate, *Hour of the Wolf* inspires, provokes, and is unerringly profound. Read this book—and make sure you begin after midnight!"

> —**Nan Moss and David Corbin,** authors of *Weather Shamanism: Harmonizing Our Connection with the Elements*

"*Hour of the Wolf* will provide the same sparks of inspiration to Paul Lipton's readers that knowing the man behind the book has done for me. Like a true rebel, he refuses to act his age—or even my age. He is ageless! He offers a powerful, uplifting, and timely message."

> —**Stephen Gibb,** musician/songwriter, CrossFit coach, and entrepreneur

"Paul Lipton has turned his personal emotional and intellectual journey into a thought-provoking primer on how to confront and make positive the inevitability of aging."

> —**Barry Richard,** a principal shareholder at Greenberg Traurig, one of the "100 Most Influential Lawyers in America" (*National Law Journal,* 2006)

"Through the beautiful rendering of his own life's journey, Paul Lipton's stories become our stories and the timeless insights he shares illuminate a path upon which we are all walking. Those among us inspired to live courageously and love endlessly will find *Hour of the Wolf* to be a cherished companion."

> —**Scott L. Rogers,** founder and director of the Mindfulness in Law Program, University of Miami School of Law, and author of *Mindful Parenting* and *Mindfulness for Law Students*

"This book is about a day; not about any particular day but about *every* particular day. Mr. Lipton eloquently reminds us that no day can ever be recaptured, and that every day can either be experienced or squandered. The book describes a truth which warrants the attention of everyone, every day."

> —**Arthur J. England, Jr.,** former chief justice of the Florida Supreme Court

"*Hour of the Wolf* is an inspiration not only to live our lives fully and unapologetically, with freedom to shift gears or change directions at any point, but also a reminder to share our stories with future generations."

> —**Craig Borders,** TV producer and director

HOUR OF THE WOLF

AN EXPERIMENT IN AGELESS LIVING

—— Paul R. Lipton ——

MULBERRY HARBOR PRESS
BOULDER, COLORADO

Mulberry Harbor Press
2525 Arapahoe Avenue, Suite E4-812
Boulder, Colorado 80302
Website: TheAgelessExperiment.com
Email: Theagelessexperiment@gmail.com

Editing: Stephanie Gunning
Cover and interior design: Gus Yoo

978-0-9890910-0-8 (paperback)
978-0-9890910-1-5 (ebook)

1. Personal memoir 2. Aging 3. Inspiration & personal growth
4. Happiness 5. Family relationships 6. Parenting
7. Grandparenting 8. Health & fitness

To Margie

CONTENTS

"We can only be said to be alive in those moments when our hearts are conscious of our treasures."

—Thornton Wilder

INTRODUCTION
The Midnight Mind

One day. Once gone, it is gone forever. It can never be recaptured.

Although it may look the same as the next, each day stands alone. Who we meet, when we meet them, what is said, how it is said, and how we view it, separates each day from the next. The same people, even if they meet in the same office at the same time day after day, are not the same from day to day. Their moods are different. The news of the day affects their reactions. Experiences from the night before are enough to change the energy in the room. What was eaten or drunk changes it all.

The days of each passing year spin away as if on a roulette wheel. The passing of time builds momentum. We look around and it is New Year's Eve again, and then, in what seems like a moment, it is President's Day, then summer. Suddenly Thanksgiving is here and another year ends.

It didn't seem to be this way as we were growing up. Then, summer nights were filled with romance and dreams of tomorrow. But as we are simply living our lives and more and more years go by, it is com-

1

mon to start feeling a sense of loss. Eventually it starts to register that moments are slipping away. At first, there is just a sense of subconscious unease, some knowing that time is running out of the hourglass. Then there is a conscious understanding that we have choices to make with the time we have left. We know the randomness of life can wipe out our best-laid plans in an instant.

We are generally too busy to focus our attention on the meaning of one mere twenty-four-hour period. Yet, choices are made every day. Each day's decisions change our lives and the lives of the people around us. One turn left or right may make all the difference. If we turn the car left at the corner and a stranger driving another car changes her mind at the last second and decides to go straight instead of turning right, even as her blinker continues to flash for a right turn, a collision can occur. We can't control others' actions. Though there appear to be guidelines, statutes, regulations, and even traffic signals in place, people so often act without regard to any of them. Whether those rules are obeyed can change randomly and without warning.

What can happen in any one moment in time has always interested me. In fact, time itself has always fascinated me. Growing up, I used to love staring at an hourglass and watching the sand pour from one side to the other, representing a minute or an hour slipping away. But as I got older, the difference between the time gone and the time left to me began to weigh on me. I had become so used to my routine that I was living robotically.

Then one night, things caught up with me.

Maybe it was a tough day at work. Maybe it was a near-accident averted. Maybe it was a quarrel with the kids. Maybe it was worrying about the bills and how the monthly nut would be met. Maybe it was thinking about the repairs that had to be made to the house and how other expenses were getting in the way of making them. Maybe it was seeing a brochure for an exotic, far-off land that looked intriguing, which I felt certain I would never visit. Whichever worry, regret, or longing it was, it crept into my mind as I lay down in bed beside my wife, Margie, to rest that night. I fell asleep . . . and then my eyes snapped open.

Two A.M.

It is known by many names. One is the witching hour. Whatever name it is goes by, it feels like the deepest part of night. That part of night when we are supposed to be sound asleep. But there I was, as wide awake as I would be if it were time to get up and go to work.

I remember first hearing about the witching hour when I was a young boy, but until later in life the idea didn't connect with me. It all started with a bedtime story. When I was about seven, as I was being tucked in, my dad read me Washington Irving's "The Legend of Sleepy Hollow." Set in a quaint New York village by that name around the late 1700s, this is the story of a young, very superstitious schoolteacher, Ichabod Crane, who comes to town. He meets and wants to court a pretty young girl named Katrina. But he is competing for her affection against the town bully.

To a young and impressionable seven-year-old, at first this seemed so ordinary. I mean, it concerned a schoolteacher, a bully, and a pretty girl. Yet, as the tale unwound, it got more frightening. There was the Headless Horseman. This legendary ghostly rider was supposedly the remains of a soldier decapitated by a cannonball during the American Revolution. He rode the land at night, searching for his head.

As my dad read me this story, he dramatically highlighted the scary parts. When he got to the parts about the witching hour, he made the sounds of an old grandfather clock. "Tick tock... can you hear the hooves of the horse?... Tick tock... can you see the headless rider?" he asked. His voice got soft and low as he described the monstrous Headless Horseman. *A headless horseman? How? Why?* For a seven-year-old, it all seemed so possible. The Hudson Valley and the area around Tarrytown, where the story of Sleepy Hollow takes place, was real. The rivers were there. The covered bridges where the battle between a headless devil and a man took place were there. So why not a monster roaming the woods and back roads at night?

This demon-man confrontation took place during the spooky hours between midnight and dawn when it feels as if the night has taken on a life of its own—the time when goblins and demons are more than possibilities. Even as a child, I knew that there is a time of night when phantoms have their greatest powers.

It was the juxtaposition of the peaceful sounding Sleepy Hollow and the fearful image of a headless monster that was so striking. The idea of *sleep* being connected to monster took its hold on me. My sense of foreboding at bedtime has never departed since.

I am not alone in this. Throughout history seemingly sane people have believed that bad and mysterious things happen at night. A man could be turned into a wolf to roam the back roads of the countryside. Most of us get tucked in by our mom or dad when we're kids. We are read some sweet story (at least until we are around age seven) and then the Headless Horseman arrives. After story time, with a kiss on the forehead we are told to get a good night's sleep. Yet we already know that at night things "go bump." From then on, no matter what age we are, we keep wondering what might scurry out of the cracks in the walls when the lights go out.

At night, during sleep, the monsters ride. Our

working clothes are off, our pajamas are on, and our defenses are down. At this quiet time, it feels as if the wolf prowls. When everyone is getting ready for bed and we are tucking our children in nice and snug, the house starts to creak a bit. The pipes make some groaning sounds. The clock ticks a little louder. Are the ghosts and other spirits just waking up as we go about our nighttime rituals of getting ready for bed? Is it only now that the phantoms try to find a way into our minds?

It is 2:00 or 3:00 A.M. when the pull of the dark seems the strongest to me, when nightmares are most extreme. This time of night is called the hour of the wolf, when some believe the wolf paces back and forth outside the closed bedroom door. Legend even has it that some men can become ferocious wolves. Whatever it may be, from fantasy to history, to the movement of the stars and the planets, the hour of the wolf is not some old throwaway campsite story. Nothing lasts this long without a foundation.

The hour of the wolf is the time when fears become untethered to reason, the moment when "awfulizations" take hold, and when the slightest bad moment of the day becomes exaggerated. "Not so bad" becomes "bad," which becomes "really bad," and then "awful." Ultimately morphing into "no way out."

I have dealt with the awfulizations of the midnight mind. Waking up in a cold sweat, my eyes would abruptly open and my heart would race. In the darkness daylight seemed an eternity away. I would hear the house and its orchestra of sounds. *Was that the house just settling again, after all these years*, I'd think, *or is something or someone there? We set the house alarm, locked all doors, but did something or someone get in before we did all those nightly rituals?*

As a child I would cry out that I heard or saw something move, and ask my mom and dad to

5

please keep on the hall light or night light or room light, because … because what? … because the dark takes on a life of its own. Shadows take on shapes. A fly buzzing though the room sounds more ominous in the still of the witching hour. *Was that a cockroach scurrying across the kitchen floor? Or something more? Or nothing at all?*

At such moments each second feels like a lifetime. It is then time for the mind to start its journey through the haunting moments of the day. The argument and why it took place. The comment and what was meant by it. The small, unintended slight that now seems anything but unintended.

This is the hour of regrets when all regrets are exaggerated. Missed opportunities are examined over and over again. *Did I really miss my child's school play in order to attend an office conference? Did I fail to take action when I should have?* This is the hour when the truth we've tried to ignore won't be denied, the hour when we revisit and question the choices we've made.

Sometimes we consider texting or emailing someone. We may even do so. And when a response comes in, we realize that someone else is also experiencing the dreadful gloom and anxiety of the hour of the wolf! Even so, we know we are on a lonely, solitary journey. It is then that we must face our unfolding story. It is at this time of night that we either become the hero or victim of our own life story. It is at this moment, and ever more so as the years go by, that the time we have remaining to make it right feels vital and precious.

No one is coming to save us. Yes, we have great friends. We know that our family members would drop everything to come to our side if we were in need, but none of them can save us. In the hour of the wolf only we can be our own saviors.

Yes, we can seek advice. Many will offer to tell us how they would deal with the immediate crisis. But they can't save us from the soul-searching knowledge that it is our decision. And the consequences of a choice made at one moment in time on a single day are ours alone.

This can make us feel helpless. But it doesn't have to be that way.

In the past when the wolf would wake me up, I would get up and grab a glass of water. I would try to calm myself down. I would start talking to myself and then comment about how crazy it was to talk to myself. *It will be fine. No one will find out. We can get away with it. Who did it really hurt anyway? I didn't mean it.* Rationalizations would fill the air.

I always seemed to talk to myself more at 2:00 A.M., probably because there was no one to call, no one to turn to. Who could I have called . . . ? It was 2:00 A.M.. And although Margie was sleeping soundly next to me, I didn't want to wake her up. It wouldn't have helped anyway. It was time for me to finally confront what had to be confronted.

So on this particular night I did something different. I grabbed a pen and made a list. I finally started asking the questions I should have been asking for years.

How did I get here?

How do I get out?

Do I have time for a redo if I can only learn the lesson?

How do I avoid the midnight mind?

What life changes must be made to put the wolf back in its cage and ensure I get a restful night's sleep?

What decisions or adjustments must be made to my current path?

As I reflected, I realized that as each year went

by each choice I'd made had shifted the path and direction of my journey. I began to wonder whether it would be possible to re-calibrate the path and direction of my life. Was a personal res-urrection, a rebirth of sorts, possible—a way to elude the wolf completely? Was there a deadline to redefining who I was? Had I passed a tipping point that would make it impossible to turn around or detour onto another road?

I came to the conclusion that all of us can either become the victims of our poor decisions or find the courage to assess, adjust, and overcome them. Make no mistake about it: We are defined by our choices. As each year goes by, it gets tougher to shift away from the course that has been set by each decision we've made, but our destiny is not chiseled in stone.

To silence the howl of the wolf at midnight we need the cour-age to face our truths. This is a solo flight. There is no copilot. And there will be days when lightning just misses the plane or visibility is poor. On such days we must come to terms with the fact that only one person can navigate us safely through this hour. The question is: Will we reject our failed choices and venture into un-known territories that still hold the possibility of what we can be?

Did I believe that I was too old to confront what I must?

In my hour of the wolf, aging and time slipping away were the devils I had to confront. Death, illness, and time were all bun-dled together in my mind. *Why strive all day, every day? Wasn't it all futile? Did a day have any meaning?* These concerns were my haunting.

After a point, it's easy to believe that age has somehow locked us up and we can't start anew, that our aging denies us freedom

of choice. Some people give age license to assassi-nate their dreams. I didn't want that to be my fate, yet I was still waking in the hour of the wolf wrestling with it.

Isn't age nothing more than an arbitrary number? My age was not who I was. Yes, there may have been wrinkles and an occasional gray hair, but I still had all the same potential and possibilities in my life as before. I just had to believe for it to be so. If I believed I was ageless, then time and aging would not be barriers to changing. I could see that a single day still held the potential of a lifetime.

Time is no longer an enemy. In fact, now each day holds the promise of self-transformation, resurrection, even salvation. What demons led me here?

How did I get out of the trap of the midnight mind and learn to sleep peacefully through the night, excited about the next day's adventure?

After years of waking to the howls of the wolf in my midnight mind, I decided to look at my road into the dark forest and the path I took out of it.

CHAPTER 1

The Flipping Coin

was born in 1945 in the Bronx, New York, with my umbilical cord wrapped tightly around my throat, choking me. The doctors quickly cut it and released me from this stranglehold. My mom told me the nurses had said that since I fought to get into this life I'd see things differently than other people. I would march to the beat of the music playing in my own head. Perhaps this is true.

Life and death are inches apart from each other. They are two sides of one coin that is constantly being tossed in the air, flipping over and over before hitting the ground, spinning and then landing heads or tails.

Growing up, my family lived in rental apartments until my parents bought a home in North Bellmore on Long Island for a mere $15,000. It was the early days of the suburbs. My older sister, Heather, had her own bedroom. I shared a bedroom with my grandfather until he died when I was fourteen. It was a Saturday night. My mom and dad were out to dinner with friends and my sister on a date. I can still hear him calling out to me that he was having a heart attack. I called for an ambulance and remember running in the snow to

11

signal to the ambulance to come to the right house. But it was too late. Even though this was shocking to me, my remaining early years were relatively uneventful.

Mine was a normal childhood in the 1950s except for the additional fact that my mom had a slow-moving cancer. But throughout her illness, my parents tried to put on a happy face and wanted the whole family to lead as normal a life as was possible. My dad, Maurice, was thoughtful and kind, a gentle soul who always seemed to want to say something, but held back. My mom's name was Lorraine, but every one called her Lolly. She was funny and irreverent. Maybe her illness shaped her outlook, because she was always happy just for the day. She would often pause and laugh at how other people took themselves so seriously. My mom's cancer treatment was a slow and painful process.

Everything came to a screeching halt when I was twenty-five and my dad died. He was only fifty-six at the time of his death. I'd just graduated law school and was getting ready for my first big trial. He was going to take time off from work to come to court to watch. He died before the first day of trial. About a year later my mom also died. The cancer and the loss of her one true love were too much for her. She was so young, only fifty-two years old.

I think that because of the stress and strain of my mom's illness and the ever-present shadow of death, I created a fantasy world where the sun always was up, the sky was constantly blue, and music cured all ills. In the 1950s, rock and roll was just being born. The music of my parents was being challenged and replaced by the sounds of Bill Haley and the Comets, Carl Perkins, Johnny Cash, and, of course, Elvis. I still remember when Elvis was first on *The Ed Sullivan Show.* It caused an outrage as his hips moved. It was the birth of Elvis the Pelvis. I would often find some alone time and listen to the radio and pretend to be a rock star. Authority was being challenged. Life seemed to have the possibility of being bolder and louder. My high school years were a time of figuring out how to maneuver away from the world of my parents, who had just survived the Great Depression and World War Two. The betwixt and between years of twelve to sixteen were a time for experiments with music, romance, and to discover who I wanted to be, or thought I wanted to be. I wrestled a bit in high school, but was not much of an athlete. I was in the choir, but didn't have the best of voices. I played the trumpet in the band, but was far from first row. Consequently, I found myself continuously trying to find my place. I searched for the meaning of me. I wanted to find answers, yet really I was still seeking the questions. It was a confusing time.

After graduating high school, I went to Penn State University, State College, which is affectionately known as Happy Valley. For the four years I was there, I'd go home on school breaks and for summer recess; otherwise I was a full-time student with all the usual self-absorbed priorities of people of that age. I studied political science and was a member of the social science, history, and political science honor societies. I also did some theater.

During my senior year, I was cast in the musical *Brigadoon*. The show interested me because it dealt with time, love, and the mystery of a village in the Scottish Highlands that appears out of the mist for one day every hundred years. One day. Then the village vanishes back into the mist until it reawakens a hundred years later for another day. As I rehearsed and performed the role of Jeff in that production, the idea of a single day took on a whole new meaning for me.

After college, I attended law school at Washington University in St. Louis. In my second year, I married Margie. My wife was, and still is, the most genuinely decent person I've ever met. I have always believed that she brings out my best qualities. I just seem to be a better person when I'm around her. Someone once told me that this is the definition of a guardian angel.

Margie and I lived in St. Louis during the final two years of law school, then moved back to Long Island, where we lived in small apartments first in Little Neck and then in Lynbrook. Before passing the New York State Bar Exam, I worked as a clerk for a firm in Manhattan that was the in-house law office for an insurance company. Wanting to be a trial attorney, after passing the bar, I took a job as an assistant district attorney in Nassau County. It was right after I started working there that my dad died.

Shortly after Dad's death, my mom sold their home in North Bellmore and moved to Florida in order to be closer to my grandmother. Soon Margie and I also decided to move to Florida so we could be closer to Mom during the final stage of her illness. Leaving the cold winters of the Northeast behind us, we started a new life in Miami. We had just had the first of two beautiful daughters and we were happy that she would grow up in the sun and warmth of South Florida.

After my parents were gone, my sister and I went through their left-behind papers. We found boxes in the closet filled to the brim with their history. So much of it we had never known. We found love letters they'd sent each other when they were dating in the midst of World War Two. These letters were filled with hopes and dreams for a better day. They shed a light on what it was like to live in those challenging times. We also found the first few pages of a book my mom had started writing about her life. It talked  about a lonely childhood, a stepdad who gave more attention to his own daughter, my mom's half-sister, than her, and about the early stages of the cancer that would end up consuming her and exhausting my father to the point of his early death. The stress and strain of watching his love suffer and start down the long road of withering away killed him.

During all those years, I was your typical kid. High school, dating, cars, college, theater, and then law school and marriage. But those years were also the time of the assassination of President John Kennedy, Robert Kennedy, and Martin Luther King, Jr. They were the years of the Vietnam War, which caused a tearing apart of the fabric of families and this country over what course to take. My dad and I would get into long arguments about the right course of action. He, being from the Greatest Generation, was of the belief that "it is your country right or wrong." My dad also drilled into me his belief that my responsibility was to do my work . . . whether in school or after graduation . . . always remember that I must support my family both financially and emotionally and never complain. I have to believe that his philosophy was shaped by his growing up during the Great Depression. It was that philosophy that has stayed with me over all these years. I had to make a commitment to the day to work hard, stay focused, and not be the squeaky wheel in any situation. Be the solution. Don't be the problem.

The years of the Vietnam War tested this philosophy of not complaining and not being a squeaky wheel. I never understood the Vietnam War and always thought it was a civil war and nothing else, that the United States had no business being there with our troops. It was a time of protests, marches, folk music, and breaking rules. The randomness of life shocked my system. Who went to war, who stayed back, who went to Canada in protest, and who died in the jungles of Southeast Asia made no sense. There didn't seem to be any order, any rhyme or reason, to any of it.

Although I was deferred from military service for a bit, I was finally eligible for the draft. I remember the physical and getting my 1A notice informing me of this. By that time though, the government had instituted the draft lottery to be fair to the young men being called into service. Every date from January 1 to December 31 was put into a cylinder, and one by one the dates were drawn. If your birthday was in the first third of the dates that were drawn you were sure to be drafted. If your birthday was in the second third, it was possible you would be drafted. If your birthday was in the last third, you were considered safe from the draft.

Fortunately for me, I was in the last third. My lottery number, my birth date, was selected to be 341 out of 365. I was never more thrilled to be among the last. But as each date was pulled out of that cylinder, the importance of a single day again took on significance. One day could mean going to fight in a war or not. Life seemed subject to the sheer whims of chance.

After the lottery, I continued law school. I graduated in 1970.

My young adulthood was also the era of the Apollo space program and the first moon landing. Although it may be hard to believe now, these were times that made the imagination run wild. Space travel! The unknown reaches of space were on everyone's mind. We stayed up all night waiting to hear astronaut Neil Armstrong's famous words as he took his first step on the surface of the moon. Space. A place without walls that goes on forever. The TV show *Star Trek* was new then, too. Space was indeed the "final frontier," as the narrator of the show reminded us at the opening of each episode.

Between *Brigadoon* and falling in love with the concept of a single day, and the juxtaposition of the horror and suffocating effect of the Vietnam

War with the possibilities of liberation through space travel and the limitlessness of space, my mind was being branded with an incredible mixture of images and emotions.

My dad also opened my thinking. He loved to read the writings of Albert Einstein. There were times that he and I had wonderful discussions about time travel, the theory of relativity, and whether there really were other dimensions of existence—and if so, how we would get there. From pondering the war, Einstein, time, illness, and death, the meaning of a day and the randomness of it all became an obsession with me. I developed a keen sense of the frailty of life and a sense of the futility of this trip through life that we all take due to my mom's cancer and the sudden death of my dad. The demons of the dark have never seemed too far away. My dad died at home. He had finished his day's work, came home, eaten dinner. I got the call from my mom that as he lay down to go to sleep he died. Without warning, without any obvious illness, he just closed his eyes and died. It was unexpected and shocked me to the core. By contrast, my mom's long journey to death would finally be played out in a hospital. Her last few words were her talking about playing on a swing as a little girl. I guess it was her Rosebud. You know, like the sled Orson Welles's character loved in the classic movie *Citizen Kane.*

All my life, when other people would start talking about a day as if it had no worth or talking about how restricted they were in their dreams, I would think back to my parents' early deaths, wanting to spend just one more day with them, and how I could only see a day as being a gift. Any perceived limitations of this gift seemed like nothing more than a self-imposed straightjacket. There was not enough time to do what needed to be done, so wasting the day made no sense to me. I saw my mom fade away day by day. The worth of a single day could not be measured.

Added to all this family history is the fact that I was, to a great extent, isolated from my family as a young person because I was so busy being a kid, a college student, and a law student. I never really knew my parents as whole people and understood all the struggles they were living through. Don't get me wrong. I knew them as parents who were trying their best, who totally sacrificed for me, even when my dad was taking my mom from surgery to surgery. But I mean I didn't know what they wished for, what dreams they still had, or which dreams had been shattered, what meaning they placed on the setting sun or a great cold beer on a hot summer day. What my dad's job meant to him. How they figured out how to pay the bills, which included tuition for my college, my law school, my sister's college, and my mom's illness.

Ever feel that you really do not know those who are most important to you?

After they both died, I realized that I really never knew my parents the way I wanted to know them. Today, I don't want the same thing to happen to my kids. I want my kids to know who their parents are as whole people. That's why I view this book as my legacy to my kids and grandkids. I feel compelled to leave them not merely a financial legacy, but a moral, ethical, and a "you can define yourself anyway you want anywhere along the road" legacy. I want them to know me as a person, not just as a dad or a granddad. I want them to get a sense of how a life is lived and to know about the adventures that shaped me and Margie.

Before I began writing, I looked for a book to give them that best explained my philosophy, and found pieces of me in some books, movies, poems, and songs. But none of these expressed things the way I wanted to say them. Having reached an age over a decade older than both my mom and dad were when they died, it became time to write.

The bottom line for me is that none of us should leave here a mystery to our friends and family. We shouldn't be a sphinx who never shows emotions. We should share the lessons of our lives with our children so they don't wonder why they respond to certain things the way they do. Our successes and failures must be told.

I have two beautiful daughters, two sons-in-law, and three incredible grandchildren. This book tells the story of my philosophy and I hope you find it of some value. If nothing else, if it helps you begin a conversation with your family about the challenges you faced and the lessons you learned and can pass on, then I am satisfied with my effort. I also came to the conclusion that we each have a story and it is never too late to start telling it. If we don't, we'll have passed through life as mere shadows.

I believe we are all bound together, although too often we don't realize it. We are so busy doing things to fill the day that we can't see the connective tissue that's between us. Over a period of several years following the night I got up during the hour of the wolf and wrote down my list of self-reflective questions, I was searching for what haunts me, what moves me. I decided to discover the connection between me and the people I meet.

My travels took me from deathbeds, painful illness, and my own dramatic surgery for trigeminal neuralgia, to shaman adventures, a monastery in the Himalayas, and the ice fields of Mont Blanc. Each experience opened a door for me. Each removed an obstacle that then showed me the way to have a better understanding of my life. Retrospectively, it seems I was desperately trying to grasp the meaning of my life, knowing death awaits me, like it does us all.

If this is the truth, then why can't we just relax into the finite time we have been gifted? Why all the battles, misery, deceit, and harm, when the endgame is the endgame for everyone anyway? How can we live well and fully with the time that we are given?

CHAPTER 2

Rocky Mountain National Park

At one recent July Fourth celebration, I met a man while standing at the chips and dip table. The kids were playing in the yard. Some were on swings and others were in a kiddie pool. As I grabbed a chip, we engaged in typical party chatter about travel, the grandkids, and his recent retirement. He commented that he hadn't retired from life, but rather from feeling compelled to spend every day making money. He said he was in better shape than he had been in years, yet each night he woke up at 3:00 A.M. Hearing this, I commented, "That's the hour of the wolf."

He looked at me puzzled.

I said, "You know, the time of night when each second feels like a day."

He kind of smiled and said, "I guess you've been there, too." "We all have," was my response. I asked him what it was that caused his nightly event. He told me he'd just turned seventy and felt everything slipping away. I was floored by his candor. I asked him if he still felt relevant. He asked me why I asked. I told him that I believe that society makes us feel less relevant as we get older because we're not participating in the daily mix of business anymore, but that I also felt work is really just one element of a larger life story. "We are far more than what we do to earn money," I said.

The man commented that we get so used to the stress of the day, the problem at hand needing to be solved, that we forget how to just be or allow ourselves to feel relevant simply by being part of a day. He was struggling with this reality. I told him he was not alone. He then told me that his wife was ill and couldn't sleep. She would just stare out somewhere. She needed surgery and they were in town to get a second opinion. He grabbed a chip, dipped it in some salsa, and shrugged.

As he walked away, I thought about the little boy who became this man and the little girl who became his wife. *Are those little kids still trying to be heard? I wondered. Are they still afraid of the dark and need the nightlight turned on in the hallway?*

The early deaths of my parents and a very painful trigeminal neuralgia that I developed in mid-life changed my outlook on the value of time. By necessity, my loss and challenges have caused me to resist letting time slip away casually. The idea that the ultimate gift is often treated shabbily has a disquieting effect on me. The meeting at the Independence Day party was like looking into a mirror. Our conversation touched on what had been weighing on me.

Yet, it seems that, unwittingly or not, long before this chance meeting at the chips and dip table, I began my journey to find the meaning of time and the day. I wanted to know what stops us, as we age, from living as fully as we did in our youth. Was it the fear that time was a barrier to correcting the course we were already on? Was it too late to

22

replay any scene? Was it the belief that as each year passed doors closed to creating something new and better? I have no doubt that these types of thoughts are the foundation in so many of us of what has become commonly known as the *midlife crisis.*

Often we experience a longing or need to recapture that which we sense has slipped away. Was it a red sports car that was never purchased because of household bills? Perhaps the desire for a more youthful companion to fill some emptiness inside? Families can be torn apart at midlife because of our efforts to try to turn back the human clock. The haunting fact for so many is that there is no longer enough time left to get back on the right path or even find it.

After a certain age, each year becomes a countdown to an unwanted ending. Birthdays are no longer an exciting time of kids and gifts. Instead they become quiet reminders that our time is passing away and each moment is more fleeting. As we get older, we are constantly reminded of the truth that no one gets out of life alive. We have to come to terms with this. The signs are everywhere. Senior citizen. Retirement home. Assisted living facility. Discounts for being fifty or sixty. Getting the latest *AARP* bulletin or magazine accompanied by various advertisements for different insurance options or reverse mortgages to make your senior years less stressful. Though such ads are trying to be comforting, for me they've always been anything but. Perhaps we are intended to get anxious about aging and feel helpless so that we'll buy the products being offered us.

I felt rebellion rise in me. My life was valuable and worthy of the full day, no matter what birthday I'd just celebrated. It was the quality of the day that mattered, not merely the quantity of time available. I was not going to be one of those people put in some elder corner as time passed. So many start feeling like a hollow person with their quiet desperation. But I refused to let age distract me from the day, the moment, the adventure, the still unfolding story of my life.

For a time, questions swirled in my mind: *Did I do enough? Did I make my peace? Did I ... should I ... can I ...?* All were tied to accepting the fate of believing that a particular age limited my choices and narrowed my options. I decided to reject that common notion. Only if we buy in to ageism does the fear rise to the surface.

A new question occurred to me: *What if there was an ageless way to approach each day?* If feeling an age was taken out of the equation and we believed we were just us today, would our fears about time and birthdays evaporate? The key word in that thought was "today."

We all know what awaits us in the end. Many great writers have written about the great equalizer. Rich or poor, smart or not, nice or mean, the equalizer awaits. Succeed or fail, death is always waiting for us all. Does that thought paralyze us or can it, in fact, liberate us? Is the equalizer a constant irritant? No matter what goal we attain, what material wealth we acquire, no one gets out alive. The moment we are born, we start to die.

For me, that was it. That was the realization that heightened the meaning of every day. It also led to my next question: *What then is the purpose of it all?*

Since ours is the only species that knows how it ends, does fate weigh on us in the quiet times? Is this the demon of the mind? Was that the fear that was the true cause of the 2:00 A.M. wake-up moment? Are we confounded by the whys and wherefores of each day since we know how it ends? Does this knowledge have its say during the midnight hours? We must come to terms with the truth of death

24

even if others hide from it. If we hide during waking hours, the truth will visit the mind at night.

How many funerals have we been to for wonderful, kind, giving people where even during the service there are laughter, jokes, and worries about a missed call or a business deal? In fact, hardly a beat is lost in the passing of a friend or loved one. Yes, we mourn. It is true we will miss them and think about what could have been, but life is for the living. And lived it will be.

Yet, as time passes, we begin to wonder if we are slowly fading away ourselves. I have heard friends say that they started to feel as if they were vanishing from sight with each passing year. As they get older they feel like others are ignoring them or discounting who they are and can still be. Does the day seem less valuable at some point in time? If so, why?

As we get older there is a sense that we are of less value. Why? Does the feeling of irrelevance get some grip on us and start to weigh us down and take its toll? The professional marketplace does demand fresh faces and new blood. But it is also evident when people of a certain age start buying in to the vanishing act that seems to be expected of them.

Must we slowly fade from activities? Is it natural to stop challenging ourselves? Do we have to accept some arbitrary age as the time to stop risking? To stop seeking? To stop learning new things? Sure, we can do that if we choose, but the midnight mind knows better. The wolf knows we are not being all we can be until there is no being. That's why the haunting begins.

As we get older, we constantly hear the same chatter. "We can't do . . . We are too old for . . . We will hurt ourselves if we try . . . We are not youngsters anymore, so what are we trying to prove by . . . ?" And on and on. We can give in and embrace these limitations, these boxes, or we can choose to define our own personal journey year by year, to name our own terms. Hopefully the only thing happening as we continue this journey is that we gain wisdom.

We can look in the mirror and see age or we can simply see ourselves as we are today. The phrase we must integrate into our view of our reflection is: *That's me today. No more. No less.* At a minimum we must continue to try. We must make the effort simply to be.

Upon consideration, the hour of the wolf began to take on a whole new meaning for me. I felt a call from the wolf to live agelessly, to live beyond the watch or clock, to enjoy life unrelated to the calendar. I wanted to better understand what each day meant. I knew I had to bring my nighttime fears out of the dark places inside me into the light of day. I wanted to have adventures that knew no expiration date.

It's too easy to go through life without reflecting on the purity of a single day. Yet, I faced a moment of truth in regard to my own definition of me as opposed to some calendar definition in the most unlikely of places: Colorado.

Our car approached an unassuming place, a type of gate most of us pass through all the time without thinking much of it. I passed this gate at the entrance to a national park. A very user-friendly gate, it was a gate nevertheless—one with a guard.

The place was Rocky Mountain National Park in Estes Park. Margie and I were vacationing there and had checked into The Stanley Hotel, which is famous for many reasons. One is that it was the setting for the movie based on Stephen King's book *The Shining.* Another is that some say the hotel is haunted. It was Hal-

loween Eve. As we toured the grand old hotel, we were told stories of ghosts that wandered the hallways and the ballroom. Something about sleeping

26

in a hotel where life after death is believed to be present, and is celebrated, made the next day's event at the gate to the park even more interesting.

As we drove out of the hotel parking lot and toward the snow-capped peaks of the mountain range we felt invigorated with a sense of endless possibilities. The air was crisp. We saw elk grazing. The setting was magnificent. We couldn't wait to find a good hiking spot and spend the day wandering aimlessly through the mountains. We were prepared for a day of strenuous exercise. We had our water bottles in hand, some protein bars ready in our day-packs, and we were excited about physically challenging ourselves.

Our car reached the entrance to the park and we stopped. The ranger at the gate, a man in his early twenties, leaned in, and I have no doubt, with the best of intentions, inquired if we were senior citizens. "Why?" I asked.

"Well, if someone in the car was a senior citizen, they would get a senior discount."

The whole moment hit me oddly. After asking that question he asked if we needed help in any way. I wondered if he asked that of everyone who entered the park and I figured probably not. I guessed it was the gray hair under my baseball cap that triggered his questions. His intentions were honorable.

Really, I am not critical of the park ranger. He meant well. He probably thought he was talking to people a lot like his parents or grandparents. Very possibly, many people are grateful for his kindness. But for me, it just got me thinking about time, age, and the possibility of not being self-sufficient. This feeling I had may have been unfair to this nice, young ranger, but I couldn't deny it: I felt frustrated.

What the ranger didn't know is that just a week before I had been racing my motorcycle across

Alligator Alley in Florida. I had taken my Yamaha Warrior from Miami, across I-75, exited at Snake Road at mile marker 49, and rode up to the Miccosukee Indian Reservation. On the reservation I drove past rodeo arenas and community centers. I turned left twenty miles north of the reservation and headed to Immokalee. This little town is a fascinating mix of a gambling casino and a working community of farmers. The workers are mainly migrants who labor either on various farms or in the sugar fields and rock quarries. As my motorcycle made its way through the town, most of the folks I saw were either on bicycles or walking. From there I travelled through Fort Myers on my way to Sanibel Island for the weekend.

Sanibel Island is an entirely different world from the mainland. As my bike glided over the expansion bridge, I just knew I was traveling back to a simpler time. There are no stop lights on the island, only a few stop signs. Families on bicycles are everywhere. The houses are beautiful and there is a sense of calm. My bike pulled up in front of the Sundial Resort. As I unsaddled there, I was many things, but I was not a senior citizen. I was just a sole traveler on a motorcycle.

From Miami through the Glades, I had wandered across back roads through a land where time has no meaning. The Everglades permitted me to time travel as I rode through the primordial environment. Alligators, snakes, wild boar, birds of every kind and color make this a unique spot on the planet. Nothing there seemed of any particular age. Every creature was just what it was. Why would I be any different?

As I stopped to get gasoline for the bike, I met up with other bikers. We spoke about the trip across the Glades, getting caught in some rain, and enjoying the liberation of the open road. I had no idea how old any of the other bikers were. We had a common interest and that interest had no expiration date.

Back to the gate ranger. As pleasant as the ranger was, and as nice as receiving a discount was, it got me thinking about all the gates and categories we face as we age, and how people are treated differently because of their ages. I felt a sense of being treated as "less than" I was. Right or wrong, it just felt that way. Based on my previous week's experience of agelessness, it seemed particularly odd to me.

To me, being asked if I'm a senior citizen has a corrosive effect. If I am older and "therefore" need discounts, then maybe I can't do what I have always done and believe I can still do. Maybe the day has less to offer me, too, if I get discounted at the gates I pass through.

Living in the now with the ones who are important to me must take priority in my life. I have decided that I must refuse to accept society's limitations and definitions for me. The list of no limits is limitless. If I choose not to discriminate against myself, then I can be like every other creature that's just living each day as if it were the only day. As opposed to thinking that a mere number on a calendar could devalue me, I must define what has value for me on a daily basis. I must seek the meaning of my life all throughout it. That is the challenge. I may never understand the meaning of life. But my personal journey has to have meaning to me each day as I live it. If I am just who I am today, then there can be sound sleep at night that no howling wolf disturbs.

Passing through the gate at the park permitted me to find clarity. It was on that trip that the midnight mind revealed itself as the self-imposed critic, the nagging voice asking why I wasn't being all I could be. It was as if I could see God looking down on me with a puzzled look and shrugging in frustration as to why I couldn't see the ultimate gift presented to me. I could hear God saying, "Remember to enjoy the day. Find the joy in the moment. Spend your time wisely." Have we been too wasteful and nonchalant with time? How are we spending it? Can we find the meaning to our personal story and just live it?

The wolf was not my enemy. Rather, it was my conscience, my inner voice. When I heard its howls, it was because my self-regulator had been turned off. The wolf was my guide back to a place where a day in a life is meaningful, where a purpose resides, where age is a non-event. It turned out that the wolf was my wake-up call to return to all I could be.

After I heard the wolf's howls, I decided I would look for mentors to teach me how to live outside of preordained restrictions. Some of my mentors were real people and some came from fiction. I found one of these mentors in a book I first picked up years ago and have since read and reread every few years as if making a regular pilgrimage. In fact, it was this beloved book that set me on a lifelong journey.

CHAPTER 3

In Search of Larry

Let me tell you about Larry.

It was quite a number of years ago that I first read the novel *The Razor's Edge*. Before the book officially starts, it quotes the Katha-Upanishad. "The sharp edge of a razor is difficult to pass over; thus the wise say the path to Salvation is hard."

The Razor's Edge is the story of an individual's journey over that sharp razor seeking salvation. Seeking his reason to be here. W. Somerset Maugham tells us that this is the story of an ordinary man. Yet the way he has chosen to live his life may have a lasting effect on those he touches. This comment got me thinking about what it is that makes ordinary people extraordinary in how they choose to live their lives.

How we choose to live our lives. What decisions we make at critical times. These thoughts have drilled their way into me. The choices I make. Aren't we all on a journey filled with choices with our dictionary of definitions to flip through, and rewrite if we choose to?

In *The Razor's Edge*, we learn the history and the consequences of choices made by a number of characters: some with strength of character, some not; some with sweetness and innocence, others with guile. We begin to understand that it is easy to get lost and fall into a dark zone as we search for our way, especially if we let others define us and our journey.

I've always found it humorous that some people know exactly how we should live our lives even when their own lives are unraveling. It's funny how everyone is an expert on someone else's life. One of the driving forces in the story of *The Razor's Edge* is how money or the love of money leads so many people astray. Money. It is green paper, a currency for buying other things. It is ink spots on a bank statement. But so often the acquisition of money becomes the endgame in and of itself. It does provide security, but at what price is that security purchased? And how much security is enough?

I have often thought that years from now when our civilization is being studied by some future archeologists they will puzzle at the lives lost, battles fought, and crimes committed in the name of money. What it was about paper currency or coins that drove people crazy will probably be the subject of various research projects and papers.

What part of a life was traded for it? What was lost for that gain? What is wealth worth? What demon is unleashed to acquire it?

Every time I read the book certain things pop out at me in the world around me, like bickering couples, clearly unhappy, driving along together in an expensive car or checking the time on a really expensive timepiece. They don't look happy or content, though the stuff they own sure costs a lot.

Does what we buy end up controlling us? Or can we put it in context and recognize the nonsense of it all, and perhaps laugh at ourselves and this odd journey through life we are on? What is our individual road to salvation? The path we are on can easily cause misery if we lose our way, no matter the social status or size of a bank account we possess.

Two movies have been made from this wonderful book about a young man searching for the meaning of his life, one starring Tyrone Power as Larry Darrell, the other starring Bill Murray. Both films tried to capture the longing for meaning. Larry is not searching for the meaning of life in general, but rather the meaning of his own life. Did he matter? Like him, each character is seeking that which they believe will make them whole. Don't we see that in our lives, too? Some people choose money. Some social status. Some want to be seen as important and have bought into the latest fads of things to own. They think that if they buy the latest, greatest thing, it makes them a person of substance. They seek the external to fill an internal hole. They are lost before they even know it.

I reread the book on a fairly regular basis. I relish traveling with Larry around the world studying religions, cultures, and the search for the meaning of one life. Throughout it all, he keeps coming back to the basic questions: What does he mean? What brings him joy?

What is our core essence. Our true nature. What will bring joy to a day? What will bring peace to us and those around us? Can we be the salve to ease the bruises on another, or will we just be a thorn to cut those closest to us? There may not be any answer, but shouldn't we at least explore the possibilities of what it means to be alive today?

Writing this book set me out on the journey to find what brings contentment and happiness to me and those I care about. I wanted to know if there is

33

a core belief that, if harnessed, would permit me to find the sweet spot where I could spend each day I have in peace before the end credits of my story scroll across the screen.

How we define wealth and value may set the stage for the rest of our journey. Is wealth some kind of internal knowing, some connection to a larger story than the latest gadget or stock offering?

Is there an intangible world that can be entered, as real as the tangible world we regularly reside in? It sounds paradoxical: an intangible real world. Can we enter a world of the intangible, one that cannot be acquired by money but only through releasing our grip on the tangible and surrendering to the beauty of the intangible? Can we believe that there is something more than just what we can see and touch, an invisible world that is as real as any rock in the garden? Can we have a faith in something more? There just has to be more. We wouldn't be here if it was merely to eat meals and buy things.

I so wanted to enter the invisible world that I went on a search for the Larry in myself beginning with a trip to a retreat center in the Berkshires. Kripalu is a place to mediate, do yoga, and take different classes on seeing the world and yourself as more than what meets the eye. It was a morning session near the end of my week-long stay that held my awakening moment. We sat on the floor on a white sheet and were given a candle, a match, a pen, and a piece of paper. We were asked to light the candle to signify the current life we are living. Then we were told to write a note to the one person we felt the most need to say something to that we never did, and which we knew we had to: to express some long-held regret, some disappointment, some apology and the request to be forgiven.

The lights were turned low and I wrote. It was a letter to my mother. She was so young and so alone when she died. I felt I could have, and should have, done more for her. The last illness was painful and things were never said that should have been said before she died. This was my chance to say those things and find the release from the regrets. It was a moment to let go and know that my mom forgave me for being imperfect.

After we finished our letters, we were told to fold them up and lie down on the sheet. A few moments later we were told to blow out the candles representing our own deaths. As I lay there, I felt the tears rolling down my cheeks. *Is it really over?* Then we heard a soft voice tell us that it was not our time yet. There was still more to our story. But if it was to be a do-over, we had to be true to our core selves. No more "phoning in" our lives. The day had to matter. We had to matter.

We were instructed to relight the candle and write a second letter. This was to be a promise we were making to ourselves. Our new selves. I wrote about what a single day can be and what the gift of a single moment would feel like. I promised my new self that I would experience life, for whatever time there was left, to the fullest.

Because Larry had traveled to the Himalayas to find some answers, I knew I would have to go there, too. A few weeks after I got home from Kripalu I decided to follow in his footsteps. It may sound crazy, considering he was a character I read about in a novel, but I was on a mission.

The planning of the trip took over a year. *Where to go exactly: Nepal? Tibet? India? What company should Margie and I hire to guide us?* We decided on an adventure vacation company, and told them that our trip was going to be a bit different than most: We wanted to get to the Tengboche Monastery in the Everest region of Nepal. They fashioned the exact trip we wanted. And so the time came to leave the ordinary behind and enter into the extraordinary. We took off the work clothes, left the calendars behind, and reassigned our projects. Although one of our daughters was away in college, we asked a friend to move into our home with our other daughter, who had just turned sixteen. We took a leap of faith.

It was in 1990 that we took the plunge and traveled to Kathmandu. From there, my wife and I took a small plane to the football field-sized landing strip in the village of Lukla, which sits at an elevation of around 10,000 feet in the Himalaya Mountains. This is the starting and ending point for many treks up Mount Everest. Our goal was to get to the monastery nestled in the shadow of Everest.

The adventure travel company had Sherpa guides waiting for us in Lukla. Their yaks were loaded with camping gear, and with our backpacks in place we started the trek. We would trek about 1,000 feet a day. Each step took us higher into the mountains. A book. A story. A movie. A longing had led me there. And it was there that time and age revealed themselves to me as manmade frauds—and both became irrelevant. It was the mountain itself that opened it all up to me. With each step I took on this trek, I connected to the mountain. At one point I stopped and just looked up at Everest. I could see the white snow swirling around its peak. I heard myself saying out loud, "How old are you? How old am I?"

No one questions the mountain's age. No one says the mountain is limited in its power because it has been there forever. When did we separate ourselves from nature to such an extreme that we lost sight of the reality that we are simply part of it? We are one with nature, not segregated from nature. We can't possess nature. We can't control it. The only thing we can do is learn from it.

If the mountain is timeless, why not me, too? I figured. If I thought of myself as part of the mountain, how differently would I behave? The mountain is grand. Our journey is also grand. When did we lose sight of that basic truth?

On the trek, I felt as if I became part of that mountain.

As we turned down a mountain ridge, we passed over a wood-covered bridge and entered the sanctuary of Tengboche. As we entered this region, I sensed I was entering a Shangri-La. We were walking into a mystical valley. The monastery is the largest Buddhist monastery in the Kumbu region of the Himalayas. It is one of the last stops on the way up to Dingboche, which is pretty much the final spot before climbers head up to the first base camp on Mount Everest.

Tengboche literally and figuratively takes your breath away. You feel the energy that circles this spot on the planet. If you ever could believe in the Gaia theory of a living planet, you would believe in it at Tengboche. The energy at this monastery filled me with an understanding that there is more to any one person's story, a larger story to be felt and lived.

As we walked the narrow trails, making our way to the monastery, we passed prayer flags and carved mani stones. Each stone contained some mantra or other devotional inscription. The Buddhist culture was embedded in each turn in the road. There was a serenity there that was palpable. The hustle and bustle of the business day back home seemed like it belonged on another planet. I could feel the energy swirling in a vortex. Everest in front of me, and the monastery beckoning ahead, I just knew there is more to any story than merely what is visible. An invisible world of spirit reality beckoned me. In such a setting, the daily trials and tribulations of my life back home looked and felt like just some minor annoyance.

After we had settled in and I sat in a tent facing Everest, I realized the truth of something I had read in another book, *The Snow Leopard* by Peter Matthiessen. He said that the mountain has no meaning. The mountain is meaning.

I realized that this applies to my life, too. There is no separate meaning to my life. Rather how I live my life each day is the meaning of my life. There is no duality to it. If the meaning of a life is in the living of it, then each day is important. If each day is equally valuable, then aging is of no consequence to the importance of the individual day. There is no then and when. There is just now. And in the now I am just me. I have no age.

There may be an arbitrary number on my driver's license, but it does not define me, or my potential. There is no ticking stopwatch on my days. If I am just me today, then that me is ageless. I create the meaning of my story. I am the author of my novel. I decide the characteristics, attributes, and passions for my life. I can choose my way.

So I sat in the shadow of Everest and knew there was more to me than the eye could see. I was one with the mountain. The mountain was ageless. In the now, it was just me. But could I bring that clarity back to the world of the tangibles? A world where only the tangible seems to have a voice? A place where a spirit world is as alien as landing on the surface of the moon?

Although we trekked past Namche on the way up to Tengboche, it was on the way back down that we witnessed a funeral service there. The procession carried the deceased wrapped in white up a mountain trail. There was a cremation. All around us on various boulders we saw paintings of Buddha's eyes. We learned that there was a story and a life behind each of those paintings. After that service,

I knew I had to meet with a monk at the Namche monastery.

After some requests of our Sherpa guide, a meeting was set for early in the morning. I met the monk inside the temple. The prayer wheel there was the largest one I had seen till then. Scrolls of *The Tibetan Book of the Dead* filled the shelves around the wall.

The monk took my hand in his. I asked the meaning of it all. He gently smiled.

I was so earnest and "heavy." He was so kind and "light."

He stared at me and then touched my arm. He gently pulled the hair on my arm and said, "You Yeti." I must have looked as puzzled as I felt hearing this. I knew that the Yeti is the Nepalese version of North America's Bigfoot and is also known as the Abominable Snowman. He looked at me and smiled, and said it again. My Sherpa guide laughed.

I had traveled all this distance to be called a Yeti?

Afterward, the guide said that the monk was really telling me to lighten up, to take life more gently, to let go of some quest and realize that the day itself is the prize. The day is the quest. I sat in the temple for a bit longer and turned the prayer wheel before I wandered back to the tents in the valley. As I stared at a red Mount Everest at four in the morning, the moment revealed itself. The day itself is the gift. We miss the gift by seeking a prize.

A few days later, Margie and I took a side hike up to a Buddhist nunnery. It was a relatively small temple on the edge of a steep mountain range. After we were shown around it we saw a sweet woman sitting at the doorway spinning a prayer wheel and eating a potato. I sat down next to her. We smiled at each other, she offered me a potato and we looked out over the Himalayan range together. I thought of the Beatles song "The Fool on the Hill." I laughed to myself as I headed back to camp. I knew she was no fool. We are all so self-absorbed. So self-important. Can we not see the day? The single day and witness what is right in front of us? The mountain range of our lives? Just take it in? Relax into it? Instead of spinning get-rich-quick schemes in our minds, can we not sit and understand that the treasure is already here?

I wondered if I could simply take life lighter. Be the light in the day, not the darkness or heaviness in the day. Help others feel lighter as they make their way along their razors' edges. Life is just made up of days. Each day we can choose to be light or dark. It is our choice. And if something is not working out, we can push the restart button the next day. That seemed to be a clue to it all. Each day mattered. Each day stood on its own terms. Each day it could begin or end. Each day we can choose. I wondered if I could return to the tangible world where everything was heavy and take life easier, lighter. Could I be lighter in a self-absorbed heavy day?

The simplicity of life in the Kumbu region of the Himalayas was intriguing. The homes we visited were divided into three parts: a sleeping area, a cooking/eating area, and a prayer area. What else was required? I kept searching my mind for the one word or feeling I had as we trekked the mountain. After a few weeks of trying to put my finger on it, it came to me. The people we met were content with what was. There were no fancy restaurants. No shows or movies to watch. No must-see television programs. Yet they were content with where they were in their lives at any given moment in time. They seemed to accept the moment as the incredible gift that it is. It was so obvious that this was the source of their contentment. In the United States, we take for granted the very thing that is the most valuable: our day here and now.

As we trekked back down to Lukla, the rains

started. It was late May and in that part of the world the rainy season had arrived. For about three days no flights could come in or out of Lukla. We stayed inside and waited for the sun. There was nothing to do for the three days other than be. No agendas. No calls to return. No argument over a parking spot at the mall. We just stayed in our small hostel and waited out the storm. We waited for the light.

Finally, there was a break in the weather and we boarded the flight to Kathmandu. As the plane left the small landing strip, it briefly stalled. The passengers held their collective breaths and then the engine kicked back in and lifted us up and into the clouds. As we left Everest behind, I knew there would be a challenge ahead.

We flew from Kathmandu to Bangkok to Tokyo to LA to Atlanta, and finally arrived back safe and sound in Miami. A month had passed. With each connecting flight, I could feel the daily rush I'd left behind me returning. Could the experience of the mountain survive in the city?

It was time to live each day lighter, but in a world that seemed to be filled with shadows and heaviness. The test for me would be how to connect with the intangible in a patently tangible world. How might I come to live in a world where honor and nobility were a destination just like the corner grocery store? Decency mattered. Integrity had worth. Nobility meant something. Could I find a place where honor was a true commodity? I couldn't believe that in such a world the wolf could haunt the nighttime hours. If we simply acted with nobility in each choice made—whether it succeeded or not—how could the wolf find enough territory to roam? I wanted to stop talking about the right way to live each moment and just live it.

The thought finally fully registered in me that

I could become the tangible embodiment of an intangible concept. I could not merely talk about living a full life, but actually live the day fully. I could stop talking about what decency looks and sounds like and just act decently. Not merely discuss what nobility looks and sounds like, but be noble. I could simply be and not chatter about what being would be like. I could be present in the moments of a single day. I came to believe that it was a waste of time to think about what a good day would feel like as opposed to living a good day. I know it sounds simplistic, but this shift in perspective held the key for me.

The question of living one day at a time and focusing on seeing my life in the context of days, not years, was mesmerizing to me. What would living my life in moments feel like?

CHAPTER 4

Each Day (or 500 Saturday Nights)

It had to be just a few days back in Miami after the month in Nepal and the Everest region when the heavy-light moment started hitting me. The flights back themselves were a bit startling. The pushing to get to the front of the airline counter to get boarding passes. The shouting at the fast food counters for a cup of coffee. The hustle and bustle of rushing nowhere in particular. Just the busyness of it all was a shock to the senses. It almost felt like being busy was an end in itself. Self-importance seemed to rule the moments.

In the Himalayas, quiet had a place. Silence had a purpose. Solitude had true meaning. It seemed that I needed quality downtime, yet I was reentering a world where slow and gentle were alien qualities. The daily mantra of Miami was noise. It appeared that the focus was on filling the day up, not on experiencing it for what it had to offer. I now felt as if the day was a living and breathing being in its own right and I was taking it for granted. But there I was . . .

43

back in the rat race. Even if you win this race, never forget it is a race between rats.

I found myself falling into the busy routine. It was as if I was hypnotized by the noise. Failure seemed to be associated with quiet. Success seemed to be associated with noise. So the business suit was put on and the drive through the traffic between home and office began—horns honking and drivers rushing through the yellow light before it turned red. Everyone was going somewhere else and making everyone else believe that that someplace else was the place to be. If I wasn't someplace else then I clearly was nowhere.

I drove up the incline through the narrow parking garage, found a space, tried to remember the floor and spot where I parked, and headed to the parking garage elevator that would take me to the office building elevator. Everyone I met was preoccupied with an internal conversation they were having with themselves and no one acknowledged anyone else. Everyone was lost in their own busyness: busy being the hallmark of importance. We had to look busy, whether or not we were. My "Good mornings" were ignored. But then it happened . . .

I had just got on the office building elevator heading up to the forty-second floor when I heard the common comment that we all hear or may even say ourselves. It has always puzzled me when I've heard someone complain this way, and I never knew why until that day. "I hate Mondays" was the phrase that came from someone standing in the back of the crowded elevator. Everyone else nodded in agreement, as they stared either at their handheld device or into space.

Of course, this phenomenon has changed over time. It used to be that everyone was staring into a newspaper. Now everyone is on an iPhone or another contraption. They may have a receiver/speaker attached to their ear. They are reading or texting or emailing or talking way too loudly on their cellphones as they ride the elevator. They are looking up or down or out, and talking as if no one else was there. The noise pollution is painful. I would think that they must be waiting for the President to be calling them about some world crisis that only they had a solution for. Why else have some gadget attached to your head and become a walking desk? It feels as if people always have to have their attention someplace else than in the moment they are in.

The contrast to the nun sitting on the ridge in the Himalayas was startling. The Beatles song flashed through my mind again. *And who exactly is the fool here?* I mused.

So there was the comment, "I hate Mondays." Why Mondays?

Is it that someone likes Wednesdays more because Wednesday is "hump" day? We know the week is "half over" by then, so we can look forward to Friday night or a Saturday afternoon of rest, or Sunday . . . but well, Sunday isn't all that great either, because of course, the next day is the dreaded Monday.

The idea of hating a day in our lives just because of where it stood in the week was shocking. Clearly some choices had been made that resulted in not enjoying a whole day because it was the start of a workweek. Yet it was a full day: my day.

A life is just days connected one to the next. Each one has its own character and personality. Each one is unique. Each one is available for me to do what I can do with it. A day is not a fungible, although it may feel that way. A dollar lost can be replaced. A day lost is gone.

I don't know where Monday got the bad rap that it has. It can't be the day itself. It has to be how it is spent and who it is spent with. How it is played out.

There is the sense underlying the comment about hating Mondays that it is too late for the speaker to be what he always dreamed he could be. Has he become a prisoner of his own choices?

When I myself used to hate Mondays, was it the people I hung out with that made it feel dreadful? Was it the job that I believed I must keep, no matter the cost to my physical, mental, and spiritual health? Each day. Once gone, it was never to be recaptured. It was in the book, so to speak. Checked off the calendar. Done. Yet blithely, I would so often damn some days away.

Poor Monday.

Friday night and Saturday night are the glamor nights. These days are circled in the calendar and filled with plans for events, rendezvous with friends, and dinners out. The movie or show. The extra glass of wine. The special occasion. But sometimes even those days are thrown away as if they had no meaning. Another Saturday night. "What do you want to do, Marty?" was the catchphrase from the classic movie *Marty*, starring Ernest Borgnine. In real life you can't keep asking that because soon there is no more time to ask it. You never know when your last Saturday night will be lived. The randomness of events in life is such that death can strike at any time.

Should life wait to be lived until next week or next month?

Since I am engaged in the consideration of time and age and living to the max each day, let me suggest another way of looking at Monday or Tuesday or Wednesday or the blessed Saturday night. Let's say there are 500 of each left me; and a week from now there will be 499. I don't want to waste or dismiss the importance of any one of them.

 It is so comfortable to say we will deal with an issue, a decision, a relationship, a family member in need, next week—or next month or next

46

year. But I am now asking you to recalibrate it all. Five hundred Saturday nights is ten years (or close enough to make the point). Five hundred Mondays is ten years. The reality being that rushing through the days in order to get to the Friday night or Saturday afternoon, does nothing but rush us through our lives. It is a certainty. There will come a time when the last number, one, is in front of us.

Ten years seemed to resonate with me as a good marker for this discussion. After all, when we are being interviewed for our first job or writing some essay for a class, we are so often asked whether we have a five-year or ten-year plan or goal. We would be asked where we "saw ourselves" in five or ten years. When I was asked that I would think . . . five or ten years? That is so far away. Or now, at my current age, sixty-seven, I would think that, although I feel great, exercise and take care of myself, in ten years, as I get close to eighty, no matter how good I feel now, the human machine starts to falter. It was that thought that got me thinking about the days I live. Not ten years, but 3,650 days. Or 500 Saturday nights. It is the day then that is the critical goal to reach. A single day has value, no matter where it sits in the week.

Don't get me wrong. I know there are challenging moments in any life. Illnesses. Diseases. Accidents and personal, business, or familial tragedies of all types and kinds. But since such moments are inevitable, the question still remains of how we face life with all its challenges each and every day. What is a day in my life worth to me? How much would I pay for an extra day to be with the kids or grandkids or lover or best friend, sharing a good laugh or good cry?

In the past I seemed to toss aside days as if there were an unending well of them. It was like when I am walking across the street and see a penny on the sidewalk. So often I just pass it by. It is not worth enough to me to bend down and pick it up. I was treating a single day the same way. Yet, unlike a penny, a day is truly irreplaceable and valuable. So I ask myself . . . What would Larry do? How would he treat each day? Larry wasn't interested in the rich and famous, the celebrities and their followers, in the way the other characters so desperately were.

Back home in Miami, I had to ask myself, *What gets my attention? What is my priority? What is worth my time? What has value in the end? What do I want to hold on to as the final chapter closes? What does a day mean to me?*

The Razor's Edge ends by simply stating that each character got what he or she wanted. One got social recognition, however shallow the event might be. Another got an assured position at a big corporation, no matter the personal sacrifice. A third got death and joined her young family who had been lost in a tragic accident. And Larry got the day.

Larry—my fictional mentor—relished each day, warts and all. He taught me by his example that the day is not to be cursed. It is how you fill it that makes it either a culprit or your savior. It is choices. Decisions. Options. Our freedom or our prisons are of our own design. Time is our currency to spend wisely or not.

I ask then, what will the next ten years of your life look like taken one day at a time?

Ten years, or putting it a bit differently, as I do now, ask yourself: *How do I choose to live the next 3,650 days?* Because tomorrow there will be only 3,649 days left.

Recently I met a man who was fretting about something he had no control over. Fretting seemed to be his full-time occupation. When I commented about the limited days, he said he didn't want to hear of it.

48

It depressed him too much to think of how fast time was fleeting. He then started to fret about that. He finally said that he did not want to think about anything else but what he was worrying about. I told him that there is always enough to worry about if you really put your mind to it. I mean we humans are ingenious. He ignored the comment and wandered off talking to himself.

That interchange got me wondering. With each new day, what do I expect of it? Am I realistic in my expectations or am I defeating myself and inviting the wolf into my life because of some fantasy unconnected to reality? When will I finally realize that I must start calling things by their right names? I must confront the frailty of it all, and then embrace that frailty.

It is time to talk about the color of the sky.

CHAPTER 5

Blue Sky/Purple Sky

When making choices about how to spend a day, I first have to be clear that I am facing the facts and not some make-believe wish or fantasy that will merely lead me astray. If the choices are not real, because some are unrealistic, it would seem that I am inviting the wolf to wander my midnight mind for no good reason at all. By not facing reality, I am wasting time and becoming frustrated by mere ghosts of things that never were and may never be. With time being so fragile, it just seems to me that I owe it to myself to see things for what they are.

I once heard it said that the first step to happiness is learning how to call things by their right names. That realization can start at any stage in a life's journey. That was the notion that swirled around in my head as I settled back into the everyday non-Himalayan monastery world. I would ask: *Am I really cheating myself out of a great day because I expect a fantasy day? Am I calling the events I face each day by their right names? Blue is blue. Blue is not green. No matter how many times I may want to call blue green it is not green.*

Painting "C.O.W." on a horse does not make it a

cow. Even if we are clever enough to convince the world around us to call it a cow, it is still a horse. In my trial lawyer days, upon occasion I faced what first appeared to be a convincing counter argument to my case, but the argument was not based on the facts of the case or the controlling law. At those times I used to argue, "Your honor and ladies and gentleman of the jury, it's a very interesting thing my opposing counsel just said, but saying it simply does not make it so. Red is not yellow. Yellow is not red. A horse is not a cow by hanging a sign on the horse saying cow. Now, can we get back to this case, these facts, and what really is going on here? You must reject sleight-of-hand arguments." Opinions and clever arguments and rationalizations do not change facts. The Earth is round no matter how many explorers once thought they would sail off the edge because they were told it was flat.

The whole journey of a life is amazing when you stop and think about it. The odds of even existing at this moment in time are crazy long. Couldn't I just see that? What did I expect from a day anyway?

I witnessed so many people living in a world of false expectations that I started mentally calling it the "pretend-people way of surviving." I realized that I could never find contentment unless I started making choices based on the truth of what is. Freedom is found in truth. Liberation is discovered in honesty. The facts may be painful at any particular moment, but at least I can confront the issues and creatively overcome them. Wishing them away doesn't work. I had tried that, and the results were nothing but painful.

The only thing wishful thinking or dreaming accomplishes is moving me further away from my destiny. There is a valid purpose for creative thinking, but creativity must be grounded in the facts as they exist. I can use my creativity to overcome obstacles, but it is clear to me that I must deal with the reality that I am faced with on a daily basis—and I *can* deal with what is before me. Nothing will invite the wolf into my night faster than living some lie because I refuse to admit the truth.

What I would like something to be and what it is are not necessarily the same thing. I must accept the facts as they are and then reassess, readjust, and adapt my plans and strategy to what is. Then I can move forward. It is this reassessing, readjusting, and readapting that separates the hour of the wolf from a restful hour.

If I reassess, I am looking at reality. If I do not, I am stuck in a pretend world, some shadow, parallel universe that will only bring me to nightmares. Pretending the facts aren't there, and never assessing and adjusting appropriately, leads me nowhere other than to disappointment and a lost opportunity, if not to an even worse result.

To me, everything comes down to the blue sky/purple sky moment of decision.

I have sat with friends and family members in crisis and listened to them waxing on about what should have happened in some business deal or relationship, as if all they needed to do to get a better outcome was tweak the facts a bit differently. They would plead that the email or text they had sent didn't really say what it clearly said. Or they would deny that some letter or document they had signed and sent was signed and sent, or even if it was, that it should be ignored or destroyed. I would listen patiently until I realized that pretend was polluting real. I would stare out the window, wondering what to say.

Then it hit me. The first time I said it, I felt a bit strange, and those who were listening to me looked perplexed. But after I said it each time, it became a welcome reality check in a wasteland of trying to wish away truths. Then the conversation would shift to true problem solving. We would start the reassessing process.

I would look out the window at a moment of evaluation and choice, a moment when someone was chattering about what the facts should be or could be or might be or would be if twisted to suit some endgame scenario that they were desperately wanting to have happen . . . damn the reality . . . and I would say to them, "Would you look out the window and let me know if the sky is blue or purple?"

The first response to my inquiry was annoyance or a dismissive motion. So I would ask again whether the sky was blue or purple. If it was later in the day, I would ask, "Is the sun setting in the East or the West?" The point was to ask a question whose answer could not be denied. The response would grudgingly come back, "Blue" or "It sets in the West."

Of course it is, or does. The point being that we must see things for what they are and not what we may wish them to be.

I would then say that we know that objectively to be so. Therefore, we needed to deal with reality and not some fanciful hopes and wishes. Because if we didn't, we would be dealing in false expectations—and nothing good could come from that. At that point the discussion would shift from trying to sell a position to facing facts and determining how to solve the real issues that must be dealt with. My goal was to help them make the shift, through a simple admission of reality and become a problem solver in their lives and not a problem creator. This is how I work with myself. As painful as it may be, in the end, facing the situation and seeking solutions always trumps some cover up or cover over or whitewashing of the facts. The wolf is patient. Once we are done with our delusional thoughts of things being anything but what they are, the wolf is still waiting and will need to be confronted. So let's save ourselves the time, the pain and the energy wasted, and get on with the reality check from the opening bell.

If I live in a purple-sky world or a sun-setting-in-the-East world, it does nothing but welcome in the wolf at the midnight hour. I may convince others that a lie is the truth, but I cannot lie to myself. That lie catches up with me in the darkness.

How often do we see and hear choices made based on unrealistic assumptions unconnected to real facts? On my journey, no matter the event or crisis, I must go with the blue sky and then move forward. I can't rewrite reality. Life is not a cartoon.

The wolf arrives only when I refuse to admit reality. Trying to live in a false-expectations universe only results in disappointment. Once I start buying into false expectations or not correcting false expectations in others, whether in business or personal matters, I wander into the quicksand of dashed hopes. I once heard someone say that we can "romance ourselves" (a quaint way of saying self-stimulation) all we want, but it still is not the real thing (making love with your lover).

Since my trip to the Himalayas, I keep thinking, *What would Larry do?* He saw people and events for what they were, and accepted and absorbed that reality. He tried to make the best out of any situation. Only then did the day make sense to him. Contentment is found in the real and accepting that reality, no matter what it is. It cannot be found in what never was and will never be.

Being a blue-sky person is one key secret to putting the midnight mind at rest. It is also the best way to live the single day and accept it for what it offers.

Yes, there will always be the unanticipated and unforeseeable moments in every day. Pretending they don't happen won't save us. It is realistically

55

confronting the unforeseeable that makes the difference. That is what life and the day are all about.

The only way I can confront and move past the unanticipated and unforeseeable challenges in my life is by heading toward the blue. Otherwise, I wear a mask of denial and the midnight howl of the wolf draws near. Once a mask of denial is fastened in place, it reshapes the face behind it.

CHAPTER 6

The Mask

Masks have always fascinated me. In various cultures they may be used for theatrical purposes or in religious ceremonies. But some people also wear masks as disguises. They are worn, for instance, to commit crimes without being recognized or to instill horror and fear in others.

A mask also can let us explore a part of ourselves we might normally conceal. Commonly masks are worn at Halloween. We go trick-or-treating or attend house parties and masquerade balls wearing masks. Then there are the comic book characters who wear all sorts of disguises. When their masks are put on, the meek clerk or serious businessman becomes a superhero or a crime-fighting avenger. The mask transforms him. But in the comic books, once the mask is removed the superhero goes back to his or her everyday persona. Those physical types of masks are easy to deal with.

Some of the masks we wear are invisible; they are personalities or attitudes. We tend to wear these types of psychological masks when our pressures become too heavy to bear or we feel uncomfortable about the actions we are going to take. On some occasions a mask lets us speak our truth and express a part of us that would otherwise be hidden or denied. On other occasions, wearing a mask can lead us down a path we don't really want to go.

One such mask was part of an essay by George Orwell entitled "Shooting an Elephant," in which he describes how he was confronted with an unforeseeable event. The way he responded to it seems to have changed his idea of who he was.

Let's journey back to Moulmein, Burma, in the early 1900s. At that time, young George Orwell, whose real (not pen) name was Eric Arthur Blair, was a constable of sorts in a small village. Burma (now Myanmar), like India, Bangladesh, and Pakistan, was under British domination back then, and Eric was there, representing the British authorities.

One day a tame elephant ran amok and entered the village. In its effort to get out, it destroyed huts and killed a villager. The news reached the constable that an elephant killed a man. As the authority, he had to take action.

The crowd demanded that the elephant be killed. So Eric grabbed his rifle and went after the frightened creature. As he tracked the elephant through the village, something out of the boring routine of the day had happened and there was excitement in the air. In order to show his strength as a member of the ruling class, he felt he had to put on the air of enforcer of the rules and the law.

After a while, Eric came upon the elephant. The animal had made it out of the village. It was calmly resting. It had done nothing but unintentionally enter a village, then panicked, and made its way out into an open field.

Eric knew he did not have to shoot the elephant. So the conflict was now joined. Was he to be true to what he knew was right: not killing the tame beast grazing in the field? Could he just wait for the elephant's owner to arrive, or would he submit to the crowd's demands and shoot the elephant.

How often have we found ourselves in a situation of believing that we had to do something that wasn't called for because someone else, whether an employer, a client, a family member, or a friend, demanded it or manipulated us into feeling that in not doing it we'd disappoint them or be seen as not being a team player? We rationalized the moment and tried to justify our soon-to-be regretted actions because we knew we were being "played" to do something that was both unreasonable and against our very moral definition of ourselves. Would we "shoot the elephant" or find our own path out of this dark place?

Faced with such a situation today, could we step back, appreciate the choice and its real consequences, and understand that one decision could be the tipping point that changes the entire path of our journey through life? One day. One choice. One consequence. One inner conflict. One overwhelming regret. So often life comes down to one moment on a single day.

I once heard someone say that all the good and bad things in life happen in the unexpected split second. A second in which everything changes. Most recently my daughter was holding her son, my grandson, and dancing around a resort swimming pool. Her shoe got caught under a loose tile. We froze as we saw her falling and watched in horror as our grandson hit the hard, unforgiving pool deck. His head hit, and hit again. After the disbelief passed, we rushed him to the local hospital and waited for the tests to be completed. Fortunately, he was fine.

I sat with my daughter that night and told her two things. First, God presents every child with one gift. This was his. He would be fine. Second, all the good and bad things in life happen in the unexpected split second. Each moment is therefore precious.

I have witnessed people who, out of anger or frustration, said or did something they later regretted. In one moment, they reacted in a way that was not their true nature, but which still changed their relationship forever. There was also a split-second incident that occurred back in 1965 when I was home from Penn State on Christmas break and took a part-time job at the local department store. While browsing through the latest record albums (yes, vinyl records), I literally bumped into a young woman who was also home for her Christmas break from the University of Cincinnati. Our eyes met, we spoke briefly, and I asked her out on a date. That moment has turned into over forty-five years of marriage, two children, and three grandchildren.

Split seconds matter. But if there is a mask involved and it is fastened on tight, the split-second action or inaction often turns into a lifetime of regrets or missed opportunities. People regret such moments not only because anger and frustration got the best of them, but also because what they said or did really didn't represent who they were. That is what happened to Eric, who fastened on the mask of not wanting to appear to be weak.

If we have done something that we know we did not have to do, should not have done, and in fact, was against our own personal moral compass, then we picked up the mask of "not me" and fastened it firmly onto our face. It doesn't matter if it's the mask of the circus clown, the Joker of Batman fame, or some hired gun or assassin—just be warned that our features can become set into its mold. At that point, whether or not the mask is on, we are lost.

When we get home and are trying to wind

60

down from the day, are we distracted from our family or friends? Are our minds racing because we know what we were willing to do and did. I know of many people who became involved with drugs and alcohol or other types of abusive conduct directed toward themselves or their families because they were trying to numb the pain of the mask they had put on to do something that they knew did not have to be done.

We put on the mask. It is the mask of something we are not.

In his case, Eric understood that he was merely doing that which the crowd expected of him. The tragedy could have been avoided. If one man had been true to his nature in that one day, if he had defined himself and felt confident in his own judgment, he wouldn't have found himself in this life-altering place. The crowd would have dispersed, the elephant would be back at its chores, and Eric would have been contented with who he was. But that did not happen. Instead Eric aimed the rifle and shot the elephant.

In the midst of any moral dilemma, we must ask ourselves: Are we the shooter, the crowd, or the poor elephant? How often do we decide to take action or say or do something that is contrary to our own ethical code of conduct and moral compass solely because we are fearful someone will think us a fool or not worthy of their employment or affection? As we put on makeup or wear clothing that is just not who we are and pretend to be someone else, at that moment the invisible mask is attached— and deep down inside us the wolf awakens.

The problem with our deception is that the mask gets fitted to us, until, in time, we become the fraud. Whether on vacation or a family outing or on a quiet evening at home, we will always know what has happened and what we were willing to do and did. This is witching-hour terrain.

In the witching hour, our conscience tries to

61

break through the mask and restore us to our true nature. The wolf knows we have been false. Thus, we become the casualties of our deceptions.

Beware of becoming a fool by trying to avoid being called a fool by some fool. There are times in which we can feel the mask in our hands as it is being lifted up toward our faces. We always have the moment of choice: Drop it or fasten it tighter into place.

Usually, the choice we make comes down to whether we are truly comfortable in our own skin. If we are, we don't need a mask. We can find a resolution for the dilemma that's in keeping with our personal moral code, knowing we will get a good night's sleep.

One way to beat the howling wolf is to agree not to trade in falsehoods—ever. Decide to become the hero in our life stories. We never believed we would be the villain in our own dramas, and there is a way to avoid it. By doing as heroes do. Heroes don't deny their true natures. Heroes know what can be accomplished in a single grand gesture in one split second on one day. Heroes act consistently with their inner compasses. We can be heroes.

It is time to go on the hero's journey.

CHAPTER 7

The Hero

Dropping the mask signals that we have made a choice. We all have the same choice to either be the hero in our own life story or a bit player in someone else's. The ultimate betrayal is to play a villain or a victim in your own life.

Let's not confuse a hero with a comic book superhero. I am talking about holding fast to one's personal truth.

Not long ago I watched as three workers spent the day laying bricks in my backyard patio. It was a long day. A hot summer day. They worked with dignity and dedication. They were classy and had great humor and style. They were so proud of the job they did. They put in an honest day's work for an honest day's wage. What else is there?

While working on the patio, the workers removed a bush and found a huge rock that had been hidden by that bush. They called me out to look at it. It was a beauty, a jewel of a rock hidden by some old, dried brush. They carried it to the front of the house to put it in a place of honor for all to see. We all stood there admiring the rock that for too long had been lost in time and space because of a simple obstacle.

Afterwards, I couldn't stop thinking about their sincere effort, the discovery of the rock, and the rock's similarity to us.

Are we being hidden by old, dried-up obstacles? Have we been reduced to living in the shadows by someone else's trash? Those are good questions to ask ourselves when we feel that we're living out of alignment with the compass of our personal truth somewhere in our lives. Life offers us opportunities to step out into the sun. We don't want to live in anyone else's shadow.

A life is a story unfolding without a script. The thrill of the day is that no one wakes up in the morning to find the script on a nightstand. There is nothing to memorize ahead of time that provides us with motivation, direction, and appropriate pauses for either laugh tracks or gasps from the audience. As much as we think that having a script would be an easier way to go about life—always knowing how the scene plays out, who wins the argument, who gets the girl or guy, who gets the raise or promotion, what clever, winning comment will turn the tide in any debate—it just doesn't work that way.

We wake up and the day is merely before us. No diagram. No promo. No chart with bells and whistles highlighting the times either when we are on and must deliver or when we can relax since it isn't our scene. Not even close. It's up to us. We are the screenwriter, the producer, the director, the casting agent, the lunch truck driver, the exercise coach, the love interest, the best friend, and even, sometimes, the man or woman behind a mask. We are deciding the day, the life, the storyline. But if there is deception it changes it all. We then give up control of our story to something or someone else's script. And that someone or something else does not necessarily have our best interest at heart. Their interest is their story told their way.

Are we trusting enough in our ability to live

as the heroes of our own stories or are we satisfied to become extras, walk-ons, and bit players in other people's epic life adventures? Maybe that is enough for some. Maybe it feels safer not to have the lead. That way there's no risk. No failure. But then, also, no glory. No possibility of an amazing ride. No look back with satisfaction that we tried our best.

There will come a time when we all turn around and look back on our lives. We'll look back on our moments of choice. When we do, we'll see that the majesty of those moments lies in the effort. The glory is in the attempt. If we never even try to make the most of the moments of our lives by being the hero of our days, then the look back will merely be one of regret.

What does it mean to be the hero of our own stories? It means to consciously make a choice to be the driving force in our own lives. One way to guarantee that we are doing this is to engage in what I call "future history." No, that is not an oxymoron. As the day goes by, we are writing our future history. We are developing the principles and values that we live by. We are our own creators. Our legends are crafted by us. Is it all melodrama? Or film noir? Or comedy splashed with pathos? Is it horror or a gore fest? Are we the hero, the victim, or the villain? We can choose.

I had to choose. By the mid-1980s I started getting a shooting pain on the right side of my face. It was excruciating. I would be in meetings or even in court arguing a case and would freeze when the pain struck. I found ways to mask the episode by either pausing, looking away, and struggling through the pain episode, which would last from a few seconds to a bit more each time it was triggered. I learned how to hold my head or talk in a certain way to avoid the triggering of the pain. I did not realize at the time that I was in the early stages of dealing with trigeminal neuralgia. I was beginning to feel like a victim. I was beginning to believe that I had no say in how my life was playing out. There was work. There were family obligations. There was a shooting pain in my face. All I knew was that I seemed to be just trying to survive the day as opposed to living the life I thought I would live. The day was being reduced to nine-to-five obligations and responsibilities without any hint of a larger adventure to be lived.

A retrospective of any life reads like a story with various other storylines intersecting it, players entering and exiting stage right or left. There may be quiet moments in the story. Lost opportunities. Broken hearts and dashed dreams. There are also daring escapes, found romance, true love, and dreams fulfilled, especially if we live boldly like the heroes I believe we were born to be. The key is that it must be our own stories we live.

Have you thought about whose story you are living? The midnight mind knows. In the hour of the wolf we are fully aware of whether we are tapping into our essence and core beliefs or selling ourselves too short. At 2:00 A.M. when our eyes snap open, we just know.

Being the hero of our own lives is not a question of being self-absorbed. A life story may very well be one of helping others find their way, of being of service to a friend or a child needing guidance. The distinction is that it must be our choice what we do. It must be our intention, our decision. The point is to make sure that we are telling the story our way and not merely burying who we are under the pages of someone else's storybook.

Heroes come in many shapes and sizes. If you can avoid being a walk-on in life, resist putting on some clown makeup to enter stage right and exit stage left because someone else demands it, turn down the part of an extra in some short subject documentary, then your future history as a leading actor is waiting to be written.

Failure or tragedy should not dissuade you from pursuing the hero's quest. The fall is part of the story of life. There has to be the fall for the hero to rise.

When mythologist Joseph Campbell wrote *Hero with a Thousand Faces* in 1949, he outlined the arc of the journey of the archetypal hero. In the book, he states that a hero ventures out from the everyday world into a world of supernatural wonders. A battle must be fought and a victory achieved. Then the hero comes back to aid those left behind. Campbell describes the many stages in this journey. We have seen it in many books and movies, but none as vividly depicted as the hero's journey in the classic movie *Star Wars,* created by George Lucas.

There is a call to adventure. The hero may have to face his or her adventure alone or there might be a guide or companion. In *Star Wars,* think of Luke Skywalker meeting up with Hans Solo. The hero then faces the road of trials. It is during this phase that the hero confronts the most severe of tests. The battle is fought. If he or she survives, there is a moment of self-awareness, and then a decision must be made whether or not to return to the world left behind. If there is to be a return, there are also going to be other challenges. One such challenge is coming back to the ordinary world after an extraordinary experience; readjusting to everyday life, yet feeling differently because of the challenge that has been met and conquered.

The myth of the hero in different times and cultures has always fascinated me. We even see it represented in the lives of great religious figures like Moses and Jesus. Climbing up the mountain and returning with the Ten Commandments. Wandering the wilderness and coming back with the gift to save everyone who chooses to accept and believe. Each had a transformation as a result of the personal journey taken.

And there is always the test. There cannot be a hero without an ordinary person entering and then returning from the darkness. It is this severe test that I was drawn to. For me, it took the form of trying to come to terms with the deaths of my parents and what that meant to my time here, coupled with a debilitating pain that I began to experience on the right side of my face. Was my journey to be short and pain filled, or was there another way? Could I find a path?

I read about young warriors entering a dark forest, or a brave princess venturing into a dank, deep cave, or Jonah being swallowed and finding himself in the belly of the whale. In each of these tales, a hero emerged. For our purposes here, I will refer to the test as the hour of the wolf. The test can take the form of waking up in the middle of the night with an unshakeable sense of wrongness and dread, or in a cold sweat. For me, it became a two-part test. First, was facing the howling wolf: identifying that which had to be named. Was it fear of failure? Fear of aging? Fear of illness? Fear of constant pain? Second, it was then taking action to confront what could no longer be denied. There is heroism in calling things by their right name, in being willing to act upon what you discover when you drill down and find the truth, in not abandoning yourself.

A choice on how to live had to be made. In every life a choice is made. Either we challenge ourselves to be all we can be or we are reduced to being another back story in some other tale soon forgotten. Unless and until we are tested by the "darkness" we never emerge as all we can be. We must face the unknown and overcome it. If we do, we emerge as the hero of our story.

Can we see the test as an opportunity to be all we can be or are we going to be defeated by the slightest headwind? Can we redefine how we address conflict and controversy? Can we find that inner knowing that guides us to the light?

It may very well take waking up at 2:00 A.M. enough times for us to understand that we are trapped in the darkness of choices made in our unfolding lives. I believe that we are the sum of our choices. If so, then each decision is another piece in a jigsaw puzzle. It is as if we are creating this stained glass image of who we are. The pieces cut in different shapes and sizes depending on the choices made. This mosaic then becomes the picture of our journey.

I began to better understand that there are major categories of decisions we make during our life. There are five such categories. Inside each category choices are made. Depending on the decision made inside each category our life could take a totally different direction. Those categories include health, family and friends, spirituality, learning, and fun. I had to decide how to address all the choices to be made within these critical five categories.

I had to start making some hard choices. Even if some were bad, I had to take some action and believe that a hero can survive the fall, can survive bad decisions, can learn from mistakes, and can realign with his unmasked self. I had to look forward.

Consider the hour of the wolf as your wake-up call to prepare you to meet your true nature . . . finally. As we unmask ourselves, the hero is waiting. A hero's journey awaits us, but if Campbell was right, there must be the crisis before the transformation.

CHAPTER 8

How Does the Hero Live in a Non-heroic Age?

Is the concept of living our days heroically an anachronism? The world is now electronically connected, yet we are not merely the extensions of machines. We are not just one more friend on Facebook. Advertising companies define us as members of a demographic, but we can be much more than that—we must be. Without heroes, the world would be left only with victims, bystanders, and perpetrators of one bad deed after another. Someone has to be the clear voice of might for right and reminding us all that the means do matter, as opposed to focusing only on achieving the ends or the bottom line. But how does the hero live in a non-heroic age?

The question was posed at a retreat at the Esalen Institute.

Esalen sits on the cliffs overlooking the Pacific Ocean in a stretch of land known as Big Sur, California. It is a magnificent stretch of land. Mountains, forests, and the ocean converge at this uniquely beautiful location, which I came across in the early '90s. Esalen is a place plucked out of time. Founded in the early 1960s, it is a gentle, open, communal, mind- and soul-expanding residential community and retreat center, where the focus is on meditation, yoga, psychology, and spirituality. Basically a community of believers, seekers, wanderers, shamans, and others simply wanting to find a new and better way to navigate and restart their lives. It successfully combines both Eastern and Western philosophies. I went there seeking a better vision of what I could still do. I needed a place to experiment with choices and seek the strength to find my voice.

At the time I am about to describe, I had been back from the Himalayas for a couple of years. The "lightness" illumination sparked by the monk at the monastery at Namche was still resonating within my mind. But the tangible, material business day of the western lifestyle has a way of corroding the best intentions. As hard as I tried to hold on to the lessons of the mountain, every day traffic awaited me, the bills piled up, my job was there with pressures of performance, and the mask was in easy reach. I did not want to reach for that disguise again.

As we know, with the mask always comes the wolf. Since the howls were becoming louder, on a January morning, I headed to the airport for a retreat week at Esalen to reconnect with my heroic self. Big Sur is a few hours' drive south from San Francisco. I spent the flight from Florida to the City by the Bay reading *A Hermit in the Himalayas* by Paul Brunton. The book is a diary of sorts about one man's wanderings and spiritual seeking over

months in the Himalayas. He talked about his pilgrimage where man can become acquainted with the silence.

A Hermit took me back to my own wanderings on the mountain and got me thinking about the reality of coming back to a world so disrespectful of silence. To the contrary, I had come back to a world that glamorized the "noise." The more in your face, the more outlandish something seems in our culture, the more it is glamorized. The juxtaposition of the memory of Mount Everest with living in this noise valley was bone rattling. So I wondered, *How does a seeker of a balanced life survive in a world of the glorified noise and imbalance? How does a person wanting tranquility find it in the age of 24/7 stimulation? How can we appreciate the meaning of a day when a day has no value in a society that just seeks ways to fill it up with stuff?*

When I first heard about Esalen, it made sense to go. Alone, I headed west. Alone, but not lonely. Since that initial visit, every January for nearly ten years I headed to the Pacific retreat for one week. This time I was searching for the balance of the worlds of the Himalayas and our 24/7 traffic. I wanted to know how the tangible can meet the intangible. How could I enter the world of honor at a time when honor seems so outdated?

At Esalen, I took classes in shamanism, energy healing, passion painting, letting go, and living to the maximum each day. I wrote, read, studied, and wandered the grounds watching the whales in the distance, enjoying the famous baths, and sitting in circles with other seekers sharing their dreams, wishes, fears, and ways to overcome challenges. It was there that the question was joined: Can we live heroic lives in a non-heroic time?

I picked up different books to seek my answers: the beautiful poetry of Rumi, the *Tao Te Ching*, and the *Upanishads*. I read and wrote. Reading about the Arthurian quests made me think about the time of knights, damsels in distress, might for right, romance, and court-

73

ly love. Do those themes even resonate now? Book after book woven a tale of seeking something more, of finding the glory in the moment of challenge. "Glory." What a word! When was the last time such a word was used to describe a day? Is the very idea of a glorious day dead?

Is the world afraid of heroes? I thought maybe so. A hero refuses to compromise principles. A hero will risk failure in order to succeed. A hero knows there is more to the story than the five senses of sight, sound, touch, taste, and smell. A hero knows there is a sixth sense, a connection to the greater potential of a life. Glory means that there is a connection to a higher power, however that is defined. The hero is a person others want to be, but won't permit themselves to be, possibly because of the fear of being torn down somehow.

Many people quietly nurture their heroic parts, but don't let them truly be expressed. When someone comes along who speaks his or her truth, lives life outside of boxes and other people's definitions, who is just being in the moment, living agelessly and fully, laughing loudly, loving completely, unfazed by the fear of critique, those who have compromised their dreams for faux security are often outraged and start tearing down that individual. This is partly why the hero is heroic: Being true requires the willingness to stand apart. Those who would tear the hero down can't admit their compromises to themselves, so they demand the hero compromise, too. Sadly for them, the hero isn't the problem. Compromise is the place where the wolf resides.

At Esalen I had a revelation. I had been discussing with the group how to best adjust to the new corporate culture in which I was practicing law. The rules seemed to be so confining, yet I saw myself as a freer spirit than the usual corporate ladder climbing person. I turned to the retreat leader and asked my simple question: "How does A survive in B?" I meant: If the world is made up of tangible, material-seeking people who do not believe in the unseen idea, how does the lone opposite of those people continue before he, too, becomes lost and fearful of the risks inherent in being as much as he can be? The answer was as profound as it was simple. The leader looked at me and said, "Just be true to who you are. Just be you."

How does A survive in B? By being true to A. That is how pioneers are created. That is how dreams are fulfilled. That is how hope becomes contagious. Stop thinking about it and be you. Define yourself. Reject boxes. Reject categories. Only a hero gets out of the belly of the whale. We are simply us today. We can live in the darkness or choose to fight our way into the light.

The retreat leader said not to be afraid of expressing my truth. "If there is to be failure, fail fighting the dragon." Dragons come in all shapes and sizes. Some take the form of other people. Some dragons only live in our minds. Either way, glory must be resurrected in our world. Each day can be glorious. Either facing our greatest fears or the ultimate opponent, we have a chance to show all we can be. It comes down to good intentions behind the actions that are taken.

The age factor had come into the picture for me. I wondered, *Does a hero have a limited shelf life?* After a certain birthday so many people retire to assisted living facilities, retirement communities, or even villages created exclusively for them. So much of the day becomes orchestrated in such places. There are activities scheduled throughout the day. The problem with these schedules is that they so often deny spontaneity. They deny us the challenge of being our own days' creators. The activities seek to consciously remove all risk from the day. But risk is still where glory resides.

Heroes so often fly alone. They may be few and far between, but we can be one. If we believe and refuse to accept that a hero has some spoilage date that will be triggered by age we can find the path forward. It is never too late to be all we can be. As long as we're alive, if we understand that we are simply who we are right now, the hero's journey can be unending.

CHAPTER 9

Age and the Wolf

As we get older, we usually start restricting our activities. What is so interesting about this reaction to getting older is that it is voluntary. We may look different on the outside, but deep within we know we are still just us. Even so, we start to eliminate certain goals and activities. Unfortunately, as we limit our activities we lose our vitality and sense of self.

Is it some fear of injury or embarrassment? Is it illness? Is it how the world treats us? For sure, we are made to feel different as we age. Maybe it is the signs everywhere reminding us we are aging that slow us down. Senior citizen signs at the movie theater and other places where we can buy a ticket for almost anything. Or is it receiving social security benefits and how it makes us feel that we need government assistance? Is it getting mail from action groups like AARP? The signs go on and on. I know the intention behind many of these signs and programs is to be helpful and, in fact, special offers do help, but make no mistake, there is an insidious effect from reading all of these signs. The day itself begins to feel of less value since we are led to believe that we are unable to live the full adventure of a life. We start to feel like we need help or are not as capable of handling the day on our own terms as we once did.

There are good reasons behind many programs and discounts for senior citizens. But often the reason they exist is only for marketing purposes. Some demographic study on the audiences to attract led movies to be made, TV shows to be produced, and so on. But I don't take issue with their purpose. The danger is when we identify with these versions of ourselves as merely an age group. The boxes we start to step into, and believe in increasingly limit us as each year goes by. We come to believe that ways other people define us describe the full range of our abilities, instead of testing our own limits and defining ourselves. Regardless of any good intention behind special "senior" programs, there are unintended consequences. The feeling of being less is one of those consequences.

This can slowly deplete our self-esteem if we let it. That many people after a certain age lose their voices or develop a belief that their unfolding stories and journeys are of less importance than they once were is a real concern. With each passing year, many people begin to self-regulate what they are planning to do the next day, and it is less than the day before.

There are sign posts, gates we pass, throughout our lives that we let define our choices. School. If we complete high school and get a diploma, the path shifts. College. Graduate school. Doesn't the box get narrower as each gate is entered and exited? I think about Peter Allen's song "I Could Have Been a Sailor." Could have. Would have. Should have. But then didn't.

Job? Marriage? Kids? Bills? Illness? With each one of these events and life transitions, so many of us believe our options are restricted so we place ourselves in smaller, tighter boxes. Many of us start to feel like prisoners in a cell where the wolf is the gatekeeper.

But there is another way. The road is never barricaded unless we believe it is. The things we want to do are still available to us if we choose. So what do we choose to do? Why do we limit ourselves? Why even go down that road of denying the possibility that is still part of us?

Have you ever witnessed any other animal intentionally restricting its activity? Maybe an old dog can't run like he used to, but the dog doesn't stop trying. Why should we be any different? With all our gifts and talents, we human beings so often end up using those talents to limit our own potential.

We never question the age of a mountain. When we stare at it, we just stand in awe of its grandeur. Mountains know no age. In the same way, laughter, love, caring, being incredibly silly, and still risking it all know no age. Yet so many of us don't believe that, because, as each gate is entered and exited, we think we need to let go of some part of ourselves. But if we are to be the heroes of our lives, each part is vital to staying who we are until the last moment.

A hero is timeless. A hero lives in the minds and hearts of those he or she touches. A hero can read the signs and recognizes that the gates are always there. But as Joan Baez sings in her great song "You're Aging Well," you can take out your paintbrush and start changing the signs or making your own signs. We don't have to permit some government or movie theater sign to change the very definition of who we are and what we can still be.

Tear down any gates that don't apply to you. Get out your paintbrush and write in big red letters: "I am me today. I shall choose my destiny. My legend still has a few more chapters in it before the last page."

When I started my experiment in ageless living it was to challenge notions of preordained losses of bits of my life as I got older and passed through various gates. Age is a phantom, a boogie man who doesn't deserve our fears. Doesn't it feel that the concept of aging, in so many ways, is a bad myth that should be rejected? Each of us still has a few surprises up our sleeve no matter our age. Why then comply by default to actuary charts, marketing graphs, or other demographic analyses made by some sales team somewhere?

It was not always this way. In many cultures, societies, and eras, elder family members were revered and sought out to provide wise counsel. They were the family historians, the keepers of secrets. The young wanted to have the wisdom of the elders. I still remember sitting on my great grandfather's lap as a child listening to his stories of the "old country." As I got older I recall sitting at the dinner table at Thanksgiving feasts. We would set up the video camera and ask the children to ask their grandmother questions about her childhood. By this stage in our lives, only Margie's mom was still alive. The children wanted to know all about her early life and what it meant for her to grow up during the Depression and World War Two. Yet today it seems like our society wants to sweep the more senior among us out the door. What a loss for everyone.

The wolf senses this treatment and feeds on it. The wolf feeds on guilty feelings, lost opportunities, and scattered families. One way to avoid the wolf is to appreciate our family members. Age is irrelevant in a world where each life is a celebration and age is just a number.

We must reframe the unfolding journey. See the positive. Reject the negative.

CHAPTER 10

The Green Dragon

Ever meet people who had everything they ever wanted, yet were filled with discontent? For them the wolf may take the shape of a green dragon in the corner of their minds sabotaging otherwise fine days. In every room, in every office, in every challenge to be met, be assured that such as beast is patiently waiting for us to focus on it and nothing else.

It is the green dragon of insecurity or of the fear of making a mistake, or of not trusting the inner voice. It is the green dragon of guilt, doubt, or anger at some unintended slight. The list can go on and on. It is the dragon of knowing that we ourselves are denying our true potential. Invariably this list is made up of negative items. It is the list of the "probably will never happen." It is the worry list. David Mamet says it so well in the movie *The Spanish Prisoner,* when one of his characters comments, "Worry is like paying interest in advance on a debt that never comes due."

The green dragon is that small part of the whole day that is not working out or that we just think is not going to work out, even when it is. Our choice is either to take all our energy and waste it on this monster fabricated by the mind or refocus on the rest of the day.

Can we not see all the good around us? There are so many helping hands. There are friends and family members who would drop it all to be by our side if needed. We can focus on positive things, like kind, caring people, and simply tip our hat to the green dragon each morning, greeting it with a pleasant smile, acknowledging that there is always some daily problem that will morph the day in some fashion, and then get on with the rest of the day. If we simply focus on one problem and nothing else, then the day will surely be lost. The only way to avoid constant worry is by putting the green dragon in its place as soon as it appears. Minimize it. Put it in context in relation to the rest the day and all the positive things happening around us. We must turn to the light. Otherwise, we forever live in the shadows.

I fully understand that there are real problems to be confronted which must be dealt with. There is no getting around that. Those are not the green dragons I am talking about. Those are real issues. I am talking here about the nonsense slights, the misspoken words, the gossip and small moments of a day that we so often blow up in our imaginations to more than they are, thereby denying ourselves the joy of the whole day. It is the unimportant, time-filling nonsense that pretends to be important that saps the meaning of the day. See that nonsense for what it is and you will keep the dragon at bay.

The Dalai Lama once said that even our enemies sleep at night. I interpreted his comment to mean that we must let go if we are to move on to realize our positive potential. Twisting things around in our minds, over and over again, accomplishes nothing except self-inflicted pain. If it is true that even our enemies sleep at night, then we don't have to worry how to defend ourselves from them at night. We can let go and the hour of the wolf will pass us by as we gently sleep. Worry prevents any of us from being all we can be.

What would living our days at full throttle as our full selves feel like?

CHAPTER 11

100 Percent of 100 Percent

It was at Esalen, at the communal dinner table, where one of the retreat leaders asked an intriguing question, "What would it feel like to be 100 percent you in the moment, unfiltered by any fear of rejection or criticism?"

He continued, "If there is only the now and if you are not being all you can be in the now, what are you saving yourself up for? When exactly do you intend to start being all you can be?"

"You mean, 100 percent squared?" I asked. "A 100 percent you who is 100 percent present in this very moment?"

The conversation then took off. Questions started flying around the table. Could we really ever do that? Doesn't there have to be a filter? There needs to be discretion. Right? We can't just say and do anything that comes to our mind at any moment. Right? As we laughed and considered this concept, we began to fine-tune it. We wondered what parts of our personalities were hidden even from ourselves by constantly holding ourselves back.

If we don't dare step out on the dance floor of life, fearing to appear clumsy, then we may have never really danced to the music playing in our heads. When we're afraid of being criticized, we are often more critical of ourselves than any prison warden would ever be. Yet, what if, for one day, or for one moment in the day, we could release ourselves from our own restricting grip and be the essence of who we could be? Could we give ourselves permission to set ourselves free? How scary would that feel?

There will always be critics. But who are these critics anyway? They are self-doubters. It is easy to judge the efforts of others, and harder to withstand the glare of the sunlight on your own life. Have we become so self-regulated, so careful to be politically correct, socially appropriate, and decently unoffending that we never express our true intentions, honest opinions, real selves.

So the question was finally framed: What would it feel like to live life unfiltered?

We know what filtered living is like. The effect of not being all we can be in the moment is clear. The inner voice does not let us get away with our silencing it for too long before it takes its toll on us. Sleepless nights. Stomach pains. Ulcers. Backaches. Migraines. These are all guests we invite in by binding ourselves tightly. Fear causes unease.

I understand not wanting to be hurtfully honest. I understand that we need to be sensitive to the feelings and challenges of others, but under how many layers have we buried ourselves over the years by holding back from expressing ourselves openly? How deep down is the true self? Have we become strangers to our very selves? What would it be like to live in the now with all we have?

Could we not speak our minds in a meeting with candor and conviction without risking offense or retaliation? With our friends and family, could we have exchanges that are not uncomfortable, passive-aggressive conversations, but rather moments of clarity and truth? If our intentions are honorable, then what is holding us back and down?

How would it feel, just for a day, to be a 100 percent squared? How would we measure it? How would we balance it? How refreshing would it feel? That's what we wondered at the table. And so, on that chilly January day at Esalen, we tried an experiment. We would live a day of 100 percent 100 percent. It was a simple project, but we had to start somewhere. We first needed to memorize a poem or song, and then perform it with all the passion the poem or song called for.

I thought about it for the longest time and then it came to me: the song from the movie Billy Jack, "One Tin Soldier" by Dennis Lambert and Brian Potter. It was quiet and I read the song as if it were a poem. It took five attempts until the song was not read, but performed with the emotions it called for.

I know this may sound trite. But we have to begin somehow to express all parts of who we are. So we each began with a poem or song spoken or sung as if each word or phrase mattered. If we couldn't do that, how could we handle the more challenging moments in the day?

I thought about the song. It is about one group of people wanting the treasure that they thought another group of people possessed. And even though the people who possessed the treasure were willing to share it, the first group wanted it for their own. They would kill for it. They wanted full possession of the wealth hidden on the mountain. A fierce battle raged. When it was over the victors took possession of the war spoils. They finally found the answer to their quest. It was a rock that held a prayer for peaceful living.

What greater wealth is there anyway? What

are we striving for in the end? Isn't it to live in peace? In our personal lives. In our spiritual lives. In our family lives. At work.

What is the treasure we work for each day? Green paper and what it can buy or peace and tranquility in the one day that is not even promised to any of us? I thought about it for the longest time. In the end, are we not all seeking 100 percent peace in every moment? What would that kind of peace feel like? By my fifth performance of "One Tin Soldier," I was exhausted, but finally felt as if everything had been left on the stage. It was a good feeling.

Can we leave everything on the "stage" each day? There is a stifling effect to being less than we know we can be, to not challenging ourselves because of some fear of appearing either the fool or "too different." But the one tin soldier resonated with me. That soldier represented me walking my unique road and standing up for what was right no matter what the crowd would say. Finding my voice. Being true to my core beliefs. Not being boorish or obnoxious, but clear, direct, open, honest, and above all else, present. Whether I am that one tin soldier riding away after success or failure, there is always a sense of completeness when I live 100 percent squared. A sense of nothing left in the tank. Peace does flood over me, because I just know I need not question the effort and the integrity of position if I gave the day my all.

As the week at Esalen played out, each day we did something different: for instance, dancing with abandon. Whatever exercise was planned for the session, it was an all-out effort. There was liberation of spirit among us that week, an understanding that there was so much more to each of us hidden under layers that needed to be released. Any layer not stripped away could be covered over with more daily debris, layers of detritus where the wolf would find refuge. So we worked diligently to remove the layers and chase the wolf away.

After each session, we headed down to the Esalen baths, immersed ourselves in the soothing warm water and listened to the ocean below. Between the 100 percent squared, the baths, the ocean, the night air, and the star-filled sky, I felt complete. I had found parts of me I never knew existed: the outer limit parts. The parts that formerly had been kept hidden because they might appear unique or not fit the current model of conduct on display. Those nights, I never slept better. I had "presented" myself to myself completely. That was the key: being true to myself, living 100 percent squared and not hiding from myself.

But how would 100 percent squared work in the office when I got home? As it turned out, just fine—so long as I was true to myself and said and did what needed to be said and done with honest intentions and an ability to be part of the larger story playing out. It was not about winning or losing. It was about expressing myself, discussing issues, and problem solving from a place of truth with honesty. I was able to present myself completely, not to critique others or be dismissive of their opinions. It was more about finding the comfort level in just being present. There was a clear difference between being assertive and forthcoming and just being aggressive.

Aggressive is not 100 percent squared. Aggressive is another example of hiding, just a louder one.

Being 100 percent squared was liberating.

The wolf grows strong in the holding-back places. It thrives in the could've, would've, should've world. Find the missing pieces and integrate them into a complete picture and the wolf is silenced.

As we get older, there seems to be a social demand for a thicker filter. It is like the saying "Children should be seen and not heard." Some feel that older people also should be seen, not heard. But if we give in to this demand it starts the erosion, the diminishment of self.

Age should not erode more parts of us as each year goes by.

After that retreat at Esalen I got into a habit. Whenever I was presented with a situation that called for me to be fully engaged and take a stand, I would take a deep breath, count to ten, and then, before speaking or acting, say to myself, *What do I choose to do?* My choice might be to remain silent. It might be to speak up. It might be to disagree with some higher authority or to go along with the crowd if there was nothing at stake that called for confrontation. From this ritual I learned that we still need to choose our battles even when we're being true to ourselves. But whatever the choice was on a certain occasion, the breath I took brought me into the moment, totally present, and I was "good" with the end result.

It turned out that it was not winning or losing that was critical. Rather it was participating in my life completely. If I was going to sacrifice, I wanted the sacrifice to be my choice. I did not want to feel like a martyr or a tyrant. No one wins in the silly games that so many people play. I wanted to be complete. As a child is totally present in any game they are playing at the moment, I wanted to be present in the decisions made in my life, to see the larger story to be told.

Can we make our decisions intentional ones? If we do this as an exercise when life is good and easy, then we'll be prepared for the more difficult gates we will be approaching in our lives. Make no mistake about it . . . these gates await all of us.

CHAPTER 12

The Gates

We pass through different gates at different stages of our lives, entrances and exits. Starting school, graduating, first jobs, marriage, and parenthood are some typical gates. Some gates, like college, we pay to go through. Some promise financial reward, while others play to the ego, such as receiving a title at work: senior vice president in charge of something. Some gates are unplanned events that change the entire direction of our lives. When we look back on certain moments that in hindsight we can see were important, we might see that a gate we passed through that changed everything for us, at the time, appeared to be nothing more than a random exit off a highway to grab a second cup of coffee. That momentary decision to stop briefly interrupted events and either put us into traffic, where we were part of a five-car collision, or took us out of traffic and caused us to miss the collision. Our gates can be big and obvious, or small and subtle. Some are truly life changing, while others we can't even remember years later. Some are thrust upon us, while others sneak up on us. A death or illness gate can do both.

Any gate we go through has an effect on us. Many times the effect is only discovered as family and friends sit around talking about their lives and reflecting on the change that came over us, for better or worse. The layoff from work, the divorce that turned bitter, and the promotion that provided a bit more money to help with the bills are just a few examples of the type of events that precipitate change. We have heard the conversations: "Jim was never the same after Jane passed away" or "When their son got ill, it changed everything for them." A tipping point is just another way to describe a gate passed through, a gate either of having to let go of some previous firmly held belief or of latching on to something we believe will change everything forever for the better.

Whether a change is good or not, only time will tell. Some gates that we go through have an insidious effect on us. Although the impact of an event may seem subtle, we are affected in the most negative of ways. A trust misplaced. A promise not kept. A secret revealed for all to hear. A leap of faith we do not survive. These can lead to a loss of innocence, a basic recalibration upon realizing that things just aren't what we always thought they were. From then on life is seen through a different prism.

There are also subtle, positive gates. An unexpected acknowledgement. A burst of support from a friend we never even knew was there. A self-sacrifice by someone we hardly know. These are all types of gates that we pass through, or which are presented to us, that transform us into being something we weren't just a moment before.

A gate that changes us can be simple. Maybe it's the first school play or the junior or senior prom. The first car. The first accident.

One gate is the yearly birthday. At first, there's so much fun and excitement around birthdays. There are parties and celebrations. The roller rink for all the kids, or the back room at a restaurant with balloons and gift baskets. Birthdays take on a whole new meaning as the years go by. I was recently at a party for someone who was turning thirty. The concern on her face was obvious. She said she just thought she would have been further along on her journey by this age. She looked despondent. She said she still felt lost. She had anticipated that she would have been equipped to deal with life by then, but just wasn't. She was scared, and also angry.

Later birthdays inspire what is commonly called a midlife crisis. This has to do with the realization that life is going too fast. There's a feeling that we are missing out on "it." What "it" is, is unclear. Sometimes we start looking outward for someone else to bring adventure into our lives. During a midlife crisis, the day itself loses value. We hope something or someone else can help us bring meaning to the day. We might buy a flashy red sports car or spend our evenings in nightclubs searching to form a human connection. This can be a dangerous and sad time, a period when the wolf runs free day and night. The gate of being unhappy at midlife is not so easily passed through.

I had been back from the Himalayas for a few years by the time I ran straight into my midlife crisis. The kids were in college and Margie was studying and working on her thesis for her doctorate. They all seemed to be starting new chapters in their lives, while I felt trapped in the rat race. I went to Esalen with the best of intentions to find my purpose. To discover my "next" chapter, but the pain in my face and the numbing medication I was taking held me back. I felt like the odd man out. I felt as if I was reduced to some background noise in an otherwise exciting musical concert that the rest of the family was attending.

The test during times that challenge our sense

of self is whether we can see the light when there is only darkness around us and the "batteries" for our "flashlights" are missing. Can we find or build an inner switch to light up the journey from the inside out? Finding passion and contentment in life is an inside job. No one else can give these things to you.

For me, the most life-changing gate was a surgery. Or perhaps the initial gate was first overcoming the fear I had of even having surgery. Before that surgery, I was living the life of a victim. I was a permanent resident in the belly of the whale. My problem started with a shooting pain in my face. It ended with me making a decision to confront this excruciating pain head on and trust in the skill of a neurosurgeon to change the direction of my life. As so often happens, this decision also changed the lives of every member of my family.

Pain is a life-altering experience. The drugs to numb pain compound the experience and change everything. Clarity is thrown out the window. Panic is the coin of the realm. My lack of clarity, combined with uncertainty and panic about my pain, added to my midlife crisis and resulted in a potent mixture. I felt out of control. I can remember thinking, *What the hell is going on here? What just happened?* It took a strong sense of self and the unconditional love of my family to pull me through this life-altering gate.

The gate I passed through on that occasion was one of making a dramatic decision to risk a way of life for the possibility of a better life. It was a decision not to settle for what was already unfolding—a lifetime of enduring pain, drugs, and discomfort—and instead to search for a better ending to my story. Frankly, it all started in a non-dramatic fashion. But maybe that is how massive change is supposed to happen.

I have often heard it said that so many of the

great successes and saddest tragedies in any life happen unexpectedly in a split second. You find yourself at a crossroads, and whichever way you go from there, life will never be the same again. The universe shifts around you.

Every small health issue has the potential to become big, but we rarely believe it at the beginning. In my case, the discomfort was just so small. It felt like a toothache. A gum discomfort. A shooting pain up the right side of my face. What was it? The dentist said a root canal was called for. I had it done. We thought that was the cure. We were wrong. The next week the pain was back, strong enough to drop me to my knees. My right eye would start tearing. Then drool would start coming out of the corner of my mouth. I was in a type of psychological paralysis wherein my mind was frozen by uncontrolled terror.

I went back to the dentist and a second root canal was done on the same tooth. "Maybe we just didn't get it all done the first time," he said. Again, I left the dentist's office believing we finally had got a really nasty infection under control. But that wasn't it.

The pain got worse. It was on the right side of my face. Brushing my teeth or even the wind moving my hair on a windy day caused an instantaneous grimace of shooting pain. It felt like acid was being poured down the inside of my face. In an effort to avoid this, when I walked outside I kept my head down, always turning the left side of my face toward any wind. I would shower, but never let any water hit the right side of my face. I adapted as best I could.

The next steps were visits to neurologists. Scans. X-rays. Exams. MRIs. Was it a tumor? TMJ? MS? With each potential diagnosis, the family gathered to discuss what it meant to us individually. The doctors started eliminating possibilities.

And then the diagnosis came: It was tic douloureux, or trigeminal neuralgia. In medical literature it has been also referred to as the "devil's grip." Whatever part of the right side of my face the fifth cranial nerve reached was subject to attack. This accounted for the severe knife-like, electric shock stabbing pain. Fear became the main emotion I felt. I ate differently. How I chewed changed. I altered every part of my life. The fifth cranial nerve had basically lost its sheath and the raw nerve was exposed. One of the most painful conditions known to mankind, it leads many of its sufferers to commit suicide.

My doctor prescribed various medications. Although these medications prevented spasms and relieved the pain, their side effects were extreme. The main drug I took was Neurontin. Its side effects included drowsiness, dizziness, anxiety, and memory loss. And these were only a few of the side effects. There also was a numbing effect to my senses. There was a numbing effect to my judgment. The day was filled with uncertainty. If I hadn't taken the drug in a timely fashion, a conversation could be interrupted by a painful spasm. The drugs affected my ability to recall names and addresses. The easy became difficult. Life took on a darker tone. The gate of fear was entered and a life of fear began.

Then the gates of trying to find alternate solutions came at me faster. Acupuncture. Energy healing. Meditation. Contemplation. Passion painting. Anything that I thought might tap me into some higher level of consciousness to better understand this horrible experience. I started to believe that the pain and the drugs were trying to teach me something. Did I need to be more compassionate or empathetic with the plight of others? I wondered what lesson I had to learn. A single day of relief from pain was a blessed day. Each good day became a gift. On a bad day, however, I would ask whatever supreme being wanted to listen what it was that I needed to understand. The questions began: Where does pain come from? Where does fear live? I traveled back to Esalen to study with shaman teachers.

I kept an oxygen tank by my bed. When a spasm or a cluster of pain hit, I raced to the oxygen mask. I don't know why. One doctor had suggested it. One day the pain was beyond reason. With that, the gate of total despair was entered. The "no reason to continue" gate was fast approaching. At such transitions, the ultimate choice has to be confronted.

But there needed to be a heroic end to this chapter in my life! I remembered movies where the hero was left for dead only to find the inner strength to survive and overcome the challenge. I tapped into the place inside me where a warrior resides, knowing I had to begin the hero's journey there, and wanting the story to play out differently than it was playing out. I went online and read about a doctor who specialized in a particular surgery to deal with this ailment.

A caring friend sent me a book about this doctor's life: *Working in a Very Small Space: The Making of a Neurosurgeon.* The story of Dr. Peter Jannetta. The small space is the cerebellopontine angle and the work is the decompression of the fifth cranial nerve. The procedure he does is commonly known as the Jannetta Procedure. If someone was going to drill a hole in my head and fix this nerve, I wanted it to be done by the doctor whose name was associated with the operation.

Heroes come in all shapes and sizes. They can take the form of a doctor or a nurse or a child smiling up at you after a bad fall. Be open to the hero. Mine was Dr. Jannetta. The gate of ultimate decision was met head on and then the gate of surgery was entered. In 2003, I traveled from Miami to Pittsburg for the surgery. The pain and side effects of medication had been part of my life and my entire family's life for fourteen years by then. A small hole was drilled and the doctor did what doctors do. His surgical team worked magically on my behalf. My suffering was ended.

Freedom from the pain and the drugs began. After over fourteen years of struggle, the gate of my pain and its limitations on my life was exited. After a month of recovery, I reentered the world feeling reborn. I joked that they had adjusted the brain fluids, letting the hot air out and the fresh air in. I had received the ultimate tune-up.

So what does this have to do with the hour of the wolf and the search for the meaning of a single day? The wolf comes in many forms and shapes. Fear is one of the main feeding grounds for the wolf. Not confronting issues head on encourages the wolf to run free. By risking it all we come face to face with our destiny and the wolf is silenced. By risking it all we enter the gate of endless possibilities.

The gate of each moment has meaning. Each breath has a purpose. Each nerve ending has a story to tell us. To this day, every morning as I shower, shave, brush my teeth, eat, walk, or talk, I feel blessed. Every simple thing others take for granted, I rejoice in doing. The daily routine is a gift. A single day is full of promise. I find myself smiling for no apparent reason. I am eternally grateful for the skill of my doctors and a family that refused to give up.

So I ask you now: What is the value of a single decision on a single day to you? If you ever wonder what to do, always consider what the warrior would do, then act with courage. The wolf cannot survive in the place where we decide to let go of fear and enter the gate of the warrior and of hope.

CHAPTER 13

Hope and the Wolf

I remember a scene in the movie *The Big Chill*. It is early in the movie, during the funeral of Alex, a character we never meet. He is the reason a group of old friends has gathered to say its final goodbyes. The preacher asks, "Where did Alex's hope go?"

As the story unfolds, it becomes clearer that Alex was smart and had a very bright future, yet despite this he committed suicide. As his friends are introduced, it becomes clear that they are confronting lost dreams, dashed hopes, failed marriages, and stalled careers. In one scene, a few of the friends walk into the kitchen after everyone else is supposedly asleep. They find the husband of one of the friends sitting there. He admits that he is up this time of night all the time dealing with the swirling issues in his mind. It is his personal hour of the wolf.

The man comments about their deceased friend's suicide and the issues in life we all must deal with, and concludes that Alex just couldn't face the reality of it all. The big chill is the confrontation between hopes, dreams, and the objective facts of the day. This serious event hangs over the entire drama-comedy. Friends are gathered together. Friends who haven't seen each other for years. Without exception, the cold reality of life is taking its toll on them. The chill fills the gathering.

Where does hope go? What is hope? Where does it reside? When hope is lost, it creates a vacuum. But never forget that nature abhors a vacuum. When hope leaves, there is a vacuum that the midnight mind will fill.

The opposite of hope is despair. Despair, so often, is felt when there is a sense of futility. It is this feeling of futility that needs to be addressed. Futility is having a lack of purpose or meaning. It's the feeling that an activity is pointless. Pain can cause that. I know that there were days, months, and years where the pain I suffered threw me into the darkest of despair. Once I added growing older to the equation, I wondered what the purpose of life was anyway. Since no one gets out of life alive, then what is the purpose of it all, especially as each birthday is "celebrated"? Is it all just so much nonsense?

As I got older and the reality of the narrowing window of life presented itself, I wondered if the loss of hope is tied to aging, pain or not. Is that why I saw friends voluntarily placing themselves outside of the vital activities of the day? They seemed just to be giving in to the inevitability of aging and death.

The midnight mind thrives on hopelessness. If we give them any opening, its demons exaggerate the seeming pointlessness of so many things we go through in our lives.

There are so many stories about the futility of it all, and of the sense that our goals and acquisitions add up to nothing in the end. But when I think about pointlessness, I think about one story in particular, the sinking of the Titanic. We all know the story. What always interested me about it was the hubris of the ship builders. The gall of actually believing that Titanic was a ship that even God could not sink. To be that sure and yet so wrong just amplifies the futility in the story. But when I came across the book *Futility* by Morgan Robertson, it absolutely drove the point home.

I came across this novel a few years ago, but it was actually written fourteen years before the Titanic disaster. *Futility* is about an unsinkable ship on its maiden voyage. The best of the best were traveling on it. It hit an iceberg and was gone. And the ship was christened the Titan. The full title of the book is *Futility or, the Wreck of the Titan.*

The best vanished in a heartbeat. Futility, indeed.

It seems that feeling of the futility of it all has been haunting us since the beginning. The question then is how to deal with the inevitable. Is the sense of futility the fear just below the surface of our consciousness that bubbles up in the midnight hours? Is that the chill that runs through us all?

For me the only antidote for the obvious futility of things is the appreciation of a single day. Everything always comes back to the day and how each day is lived. The paradox is that by not living each day to its full potential, no matter our age, and by only focusing on the endgame, we do not really live any single day. All we do, then, is fret.

We should set goals, but it is the day's adventure that must be appreciated.

Where does hope reside? It is an inside job. The day is not futile. The day has meaning. The day is there for the taking. If you doubt these words, focus on nature. You'll see it is forever growing, changing, blooming, fading, and blooming again. Beauty is everywhere.

The real question is: How do we choose to fill the one single day we've got? It can't be taken for granted.

101

I once teased a dear friend, who always fretted about everything, that maybe if she fretted just a bit more she could assure herself that she'd live forever. She stared at me, laughed, and agreed that her worry accomplished nothing except giving her frown lines. So, I asked, "If the great equalizer is waiting for you anyway, don't you think it makes sense to really enjoy the moment?"

A friend reaching out to another friend is not pointless. A loving journey together, trying to fill each day with seeing the sights and sounds of nature, is not pointless. Holding your grandchild and praying that he or she can find peace in the quiet moments of the day has value. Being the light for others who might be experiencing the belly-of-the-whale moment, like Jonah in the Bible, has purpose. Emotions are not futile. Love is not wasteful. Being present for each other is an ageless experience. Such occasions are timeless. The day itself knows no boundary. The choice we make of how to fill the day can either be the barrier to experiencing a full and rich life or it can be an open field of possibilities.

At night it is so easy to let the mind race, to cry out for some larger meaning, wondering, *What is the meaning of life?* We don't recognize that the meaning of life is how we choose to live each day. We don't have to go looking for meaning. It's already here. There is no duality. Each day stands alone. Rather than fill it with despair, you can fill it with a promise to yourself that you are going to enjoy the hell out of it.

The Garden of Eden is here and now if we can just believe that it is our creation. Why would we choose hell when the Garden is within our reach? All we have to do is open our arms and embrace it. The Garden is not some place we go to after our lives are over. It is not some long ago and faraway land in a biblical story. The Garden is within our hearts. It is a place we can choose to live in now.

We are in the creation business. We create the world we want to live in. We create a hopeful world or a tortured one. But make no mistake about it, the world is our creation. Titanic events happen. Life can be unpredictable and make us feel helpless. Even so, we can acknowledge the uncertainty of it all and simply decide that the moment has value and each day is to be lived completely in spite of, or even, because of that very uncertainty.

If we believe and decide that age and time are not barriers to our power of creativity, then we also know it is never too late to change direction, adjust the sunglasses, and head toward the light. A single day is the solution to any feeling of despair.

Understanding this is what led me to Everest.

CHAPTER 14

There Is Always a High Noon

The train was scheduled to arrive at noon in Hadleyville, a peaceful town in the New Mexico territory in the 1870s. Normally that would not be news. The train always came in at noon. But on this particular day, three events were going to collide. The marshal, Will Kane, was getting married and the entire town would be in the church for the grand occasion, a morning ceremony. Joy filled the air. This was also the last day that Kane was to be the town's marshal. He was retiring from the tough job of keeping peace. The new marshal had not yet arrived, but that didn't seem to be of any concern to the quiet town. Of course, none of the townspeople was aware that, at that very moment, the noon train was bringing a gunslinger to town. That bad guy's arrival was the third event.

Frank Miller had just been released from prison. He was a vicious criminal who Marshal Kane had put away years earlier. But on this very day of the marshal's wedding celebration, Miller, a man who'd vowed to

105

get vengeance on the marshal, was arriving to meet up with his gang and murder Will Kane.

What to do? Will was getting married. He was retiring and leaving town right after the ceremony. When everyone learned about the noon train passenger, the town leaders wanted Will to leave. They believed that if he was not there, then there would be no violence.

Have we all been there? I don't mean facing down some killer, but facing down some old nemesis, whether in the form of a person or a tough choice that has to be made. What is our Frank Miller moment? Is it an addiction? A compulsion? An uncontrollable desire? A toxic work place? An abusive relationship? In such a moment, we are forced to decide which way to go or action to take.

We may believe that by putting off the choice we can evade it completely. We could either take the easy way, by just moving on and rationalizing our behavior, or the tougher way of finally facing our fears and meeting our nemesis head on, once and for all. Although we may think someone will come to save us, in the end, we know it is our choice and our action alone that will decide our destiny.

In Hadleyville, no one was coming to assist Will. For whatever reason, and there were many, no one came forward. Either it was not their job or it was too risky or they had the delusional belief that if there was no opposition to evil there would be no evil.

We have seen this type of reaction before. We try to appease our way out of a challenge even when we know that appeasement will not work. Even if we close our eyes, the devil is still there.

So no one stepped forward. "It is not my responsibility," was the common cry of the townspeople as the marshal tried to deputize them.

106

"Why me? Don't come to me."

That's a typical reaction. When high noon comes in their lives, some people will say that they would rather live in fear than risk harm. What they don't realize is that living in fear does harm over and over again.

Of course, the hero doesn't have the choice to ignore the decision. The moment is coming, ready or not. The marshal thinks of leaving, but decides to stay. He understood that a day of appeasement is filled with constant worry and slinking around in order to avoid confronting danger. We must face our issues, no matter what they may be, in order to open the path to a promise we make to ourselves, a promise of living a life of worth and value. Whether it is finally leaving that job that is never going to tap your full potential or seek out a loving relationship as opposed to a suffocating one or finally having that surgery, the moment must be seized.

Once again, no one comes to save the hero. It is a solo job.

Kane does not run. Maybe because he knows you cannot outrun fear. I heard a Zen Buddhist phrase a long time ago that speaks to this: "Wherever you go, there you are." Kane knows that wherever he and his new bride go, there will be either Frank Miller or a Frank Miller type to face or continue to run from. And so, on the dusty streets of Hadleyville, a single man faces down a gang of killers.

Everyone else waits and watches from the shadows. They believe they are safe living in the corners of town and with doors locked, staring out from behind their curtains, but without a hero to act on their behalf, they are really only putting off the inevitable confrontation. As they hide, they lose all sense of the true purpose of the day. Their day becomes nothing more than watching the hands of the clock tick down and their life tick away. Sooner or later, your nemesis must be faced.

Have you ever put off a tough choice believing you've actually made a decision? That is the true moment of purple sky in a blue sky world. It's a lot like being one of those frightened townspeople. However, you can't hide forever. Reality must be faced.

The moment of confrontation plays out at high noon.

The movie *High Noon,* starring Gary Cooper as the marshal and Grace Kelly as his young bride, was riveting to me as a seven-year old boy. Since then, it has lingered with me for a lifetime, that we alone must confront our fears. Fear doesn't go away if we ignore it. It just gets stronger and stronger, tainting every other relationship and aspect of our lives. No. Fear must be faced. If not, the howl of the wolf will surely be there . . . perhaps not at noon, but twelve hours later at midnight. Years later I read that the movie was intended as an allegory of those who had the courage to confront the House Un-American Activities Committee during the McCarthy era. So many, fearful of having their livelihood adversely affected, did nothing. A few turned to face the conflict head on.

Hiding leads to despair. Hope is achieved in addressing our challenges head on. Success or failure is not as important as the decision not to hide. No one really knows what they mean until long after the story is over. Only in the final pages of any book, the final minutes of any movie, or the later years of our lives, do we really know which turn in the road led to something good and which to lost opportunities.

We have all been to glorious weddings. The bride and groom are blissful, and we all agree this union was meant to be. Yet years later, during the same couple's bitter divorce we ponder the failure of their relationship. Or maybe we plan a wonderful vacation only to be on the wrong plane at the wrong time that goes down. Only time tells us what worked and what didn't work. Therefore our honest intentions in the moment are the only reality worth our attention.

High noon can happen at any time of the day or night. The "dusty streets" could be a sterile operating room or a polished mahogany corporate boardroom. It could be a courtroom or a family gathering where a secret must finally be dealt with. High noon is that time when the decision to stop running by denying the reality of what is must be made.

I often think about the effect that story had on me. Why was its imprint so powerful and deep? I saw it in a movie theater and was impressed. I watched as the hero faced down and then killed the outlaws. The town hid, except for Will's wife, who came back from the outgoing train to help him. Maybe it was that part of a family member being there in the time of crisis that also affected me so.

Upon reflection, I finally realized that the story impressed me so deeply because it was tied into comments my mom and dad used to tell me growing up. My dad would always say, "When the going gets tough, the tough get going." He explained to me that when life throws us curve balls and something gets difficult it is the time to be tough and face it down then and there.

My mom would always say, "When it is tight for others, it is just right for us." To her, this meant, that I was built for challenge. Part of my destiny was to be in tight situations, such as taking a leap of faith to not only go for my surgery, but also to embrace the challenge. Tight situations are just a state of mind.

I suppose that their philosophy came from them having to deal with my mom's brutal cancer for most of their married life. It was at a time when bone marrow transplants were not possible. So the alternatives were a mixed bag of treatments. One such treatment was a splenectomy. The doctors removed my mom's spleen in an effort to do something with her defective blood cells that I never quite understood. By their example and their words, they taught me to stand up and face the obstacle. I got the message, "Don't turn away."

My parents went from doctor to doctor, surgery to surgery, always with a smile on their faces or a soft chuckle. It was as if they understood the constant challenges in life. To them, my mother's cancer was a test of their will power. They understood that what was relevant, through all the surgeries and treatments, was that there was a choice to be made: Sink into despair and the futility of it all, or move toward the light and be hopeful.

My parents taught me that in tough times I was to stay tough and find joy in each day. But I didn't really grasp, until after my dad died, that it was a struggle to remain hopeful. I didn't know how much stress the situation put on them. They made it look so easy, when it was really tough. They dealt with it late at night in private where my sister and I couldn't see. Each night my dad would drink wine and take sleeping pills.

Looking back on it now, I guess denial and self-medication was the only way he could deal with my mom's illness. I have come to understand that each day in my parents' lives was so stressful and frightening that they coped the best way they knew how.

Before my mother succumbed to the cancer, my dad had a massive heart attack and died in his sleep. Was the cause the stress that was just too much for him to handle or was it a little too much wine and sleeping pills that he took that one night? Was his death a terrible accident? He was only fifty-six years old when he died. He left behind my mom, now a fifty-two-year old woman dying of cancer.

Although she somehow seemed to appreciate the days she had left, she was also haunted by wondering about the real cause of my dad's death.

Their struggles and deaths taught me the need to address events openly, honestly, and clearly. Hiding from a challenge or not being able to cope with it only delays the inevitable. My dad's death also taught me lessons on commitment and the true meaning of love. He had grown up during the Great Depression. That was a generation that knew great challenges. By virtue of the onset of the war in Europe, the economic hardships, and the daily struggle to find a sliver of joy in a frightening world, each day had its high drama.

My dad was the manager of a dairy. Each morning at 4:00 A.M. he would don his brown uniform with the company logo on it and head off to work. His job was to get the milk trucks ready for their deliveries and make certain the plant was operating efficiently. He truly believed that the trucks could not make their appointed rounds unless he was there to oversee the process. Thus, he rarely took a day off. He rarely went on vacation. He just knew that he had to be there to make certain the plant hummed smoothly throughout the day.

About 5:00 P.M. or so, after a twelve-hour day and having scheduled the next day's routes and products to be delivered, he came home. After dinner, he would climb the steps up to the little room next to their bedroom, put on Perry Como singing "It's Impossible" or Lynn Anderson's "I Never Promised You a Rose Garden," have his glass of wine, and shortly before bed, take the sleeping pill. In the evenings, he also liked to read. He would read a bit about the life of Albert Einstein, the theory of relativity, and the possibility of time travel. He studied different religions, and I have no doubt he

111

would get lost in dreams of what could have been. Because he had to help support his family during the Great Depression, he settled for a two-year college degree instead of going on to medical school. It seems that he was always searching for the meaning of each day. Was there something larger and grander?

So at fifty-six years of age he was gone. At fifty-two years of age my mom found herself a widow and dying. She tried to fight sinking into uncontrollable despair. It was hard. It was sad. How easy it would have been for her to get trapped in a Hadleyville of the mind.

I keep thinking of how all our lives start out with such promise, but then how circumstances, decisions, fate, randomness either assist us in fulfilling that promise or in shattering it. Life is like a flipping coin hitting the ground and spinning around again.

Mom would often comment, "Man plans and God laughs." When I asked her what she meant by that, she would shrug and say, "Paul, it is the day. I am just trying to get through the day. We are not promised anything more." She would also say that these were the cards she was dealt and each day had to be viewed as a gift, each moment a blessing, each friend cherished, each sunrise and sunset honored. That is what she tried to do for the next year, before it was finally time for her to let go.

The early deaths of my mom and dad were a tipping point for me. The frailty of life registered deeply. I could see that the gift we are presented with was clearly too precious to toss around casually. The biggest lesson I learned was that the most valuable currency we have is not money or any coin of any realm, but time. Time is the currency of value. Maybe that is why damning Mondays or any other day literally offends me.

What I would give for another Monday with either of my parents! They both lived with an appreciation of each moment they had with each other and with their children. They tried to cope as best as they could. They tried to find some grace in the day.

Once the battle was over and Frank Miller and his gang lay dead on those streets, the citizens of the town came out to see what happened. As they looked around, you could sense their shame. Will tossed his badge onto the ground and placed his new bride in the horse drawn buggy and quietly rode out of town. Not a word was spoken. It was a graceful exit after a harrowing ordeal.

Living in a state of grace seems to be the antidote to a sense of futility and the frailty of life. But is that a choice we can make? I feel we must try. I believe it is in our power to choose to live in a state of grace or despair. High noon. I know the wolf cannot survive in any territory where grace lives.

CHAPTER 15

The Rhino

Shamanism has always interested me. To read about those who could enter some altered state of consciousness and become one with the world of the spirits has fascinated me. Maybe it was the early movies or stories about the medicine men and women of the Native American cultures that first brought them to my attention. I read about shape shifting and wondered how it would feel to be transformed. To be able to let go of the concrete world and enter the world of the invisible and intangible was what I wanted to do. So when I read about a shamanic retreat that was being held at Esalen, I jumped at the chance to delve into this world first hand.

We sat in the sacred circle. The setting was in a building known as the Big House. This is a mansion sitting on the very edge of a cliff overlooking the Pacific. The wall-sized glass windows in the room where we were seated let us see nature in all her power and glory as we started the visualization of our journey to the lower world.

There are three worlds in shamanism: the upper world, the lower world, and the middle world.

All are believed to be real, though some are non-ordinary.

The smudge bundle was lit and I could smell and feel the herbs as its smoke filled the air and my being. The drums had reached that point in their pounding where I felt as if I were back in the womb listening to my mother's heartbeat. I was deep into the visualization. Calm descended over me and I was transported to an altered universe as the shaman teachers had said would happen.

The lower world is where I journeyed to meet my power animal and other spirit guides. I traveled to this world through a hole in nature. This can be done through some cave or mountain crevice, a tree opening, or a hidden entrance behind a waterfall. Once I entered my opening in the earth, I slowly descended, one layer at a time, gently going deeper and deeper into my soulful search. The vision quest was in full-gear by the time I was asked to locate my power animal. Whether I initially believed it or not, I was told that I had one. Many animals would likely appear, but if one showed itself to me three times that would be the one.

Our power animals waited to be discovered.

It was explained that the power animal I would meet was to help me find my way back to my center and give me strength during the challenging times in my life. It would be able to help me choose which path to take as I entered or exited difficult gates on my life's journey.

I've always felt a connection to certain animals and didn't know why. Certain animals have just resonated with me. That day, during my journey to the lower world, one animal did reveal itself three times to me. This animal was one I had never really thought about before. But there it was. I thought maybe my power animal would be a lion or bear or eagle, as they are so romantic and beautiful to watch at rest or in action. But it was none of them. Instead, it was the rhino.

The rhino. *Really?* I tried to fight the fact that it had appeared three times. I kept looking for some other more graceful, gallant creature. But there was the rhino, over and over and over again. It was present as clearly as if I were visiting the zoo or had come across it in some natural setting. The rhino. Big. Massive body. Magnificent horn. Solid. Stable. Present.

After I returned from the lower-world visualization, I sat with the other seekers in the group and we talked about our animal guides and their particular meanings. The shamans explained what each animal signified and how it matched the particular journey we were on. They said if I followed my power animal's characteristics I would learn lessons and grow in ways I had never imagined. So I began to examine the rhino and tried to find its connection with me and my journey.

The rhino is almost entirely blind. Yet the species has survived for millions of years. How? What did it know that I needed to know? I learned that the rhino enjoys contemplative solitude. That seemed to be what I so longed for and always enjoyed: alone time. In our discussion, the shamans said they believed the rhino was telling me to appreciate each moment. It wanted me to know that the day has value standing all alone in its own twenty-four-hour space. Monday or Saturday, the rhino is comfortable in its own skin.

I learned that the rhino savors the connection it has to the earth. It is solid and has great energy, which it uses only when needed. It knows how to preserve its strength. But it was the rhino horn and its location that fascinated me. Although I had studied the chakra system years before, only through consideration of the rhino did the information start to register.

Chakras are centers in the body where a person collects energy. There are seven primary chakras in the human body. The root chakra located at the base of the spine, the sacral chakra found in the lower abdomen, the solar plexus chakra located in the upper abdomen, the heart chakra, the throat chakra, the third-eye chakra found in the forehead between the eyes, and the crown chakra located at the very tip of the head.

The rhino horn sits between the rhino's third-eye chakra and its throat chakra. This combination is powerful. Whether I believed in the chakras or not, both of these chakras pertain to intuition, clear communication, honesty in relationships, and an understanding that there is more to us than the five senses. I felt there was a sixth sense I was being invited to embrace, a power beyond my abilities of sight, sound, taste, touch, and smell. A belief in this would permit me to close of my eyes and open my heart and soul to the more of me.

As a power animal, the rhino could teach me to stay calm and focused. It could teach me not to make judgment calls based on what I may first see, because it could teach me that there is always more going on than what my eyes showed me. I have always been interested in the story behind the main story and the small moments in a life that somehow forever affect the more obvious storyline. Just as the intersecting lines and different threads of a fabric create the whole fabric, my life was a mixture of events and meaning. My intuition and instincts helped me navigate the mix that is my life.

The back story of any story is where so many of its answers lie. Could I see the part of the story that was not immediately revealed? The layer of life that was not so obvious yet was its driving force? I began to see that the onion skin must constantly be peeled back to find the true meaning of events. The uncertainty of how events play out is what has always made the singular moment so vital to me. There is just no guarantee from moment to moment. Finding the calm rhino as my power animal gave me a sense of being able to contemplate the beauty of the moment even in its uncertainty. My ultimate discovery was that the random intertwining of lives is what makes each moment so exhilarating. People I'd never even met could affect my life. So I had to remain open to this unfolding possibility.

Hearing what the shamans said about the rhino, I wanted to embrace the concept that there was more to me and my surroundings than I could ever truly understand. That acceptance would open the doorway for seeing beyond any mini-drama in my day and would open up the possibilities of what could still be. I started to see myself as more than just the sum of my parts. I saw that I am part of the larger story. I can effect change in myself and others. That is a certainty simply because of the intersecting of choices and lives. I saw that I had the opportunity to be part of the ebb and flow of the whole story.

Following my return from the lower world, I wrote in my journal about how I had realized that we are each beautiful in our own special way. That seemed to be a key for me: We must focus on the beauty of our differences, the beauty of our imperfections. Sameness would be so dull. Therefore change and difference must be welcomed into our lives. We are each perfect in our own imperfect way.

The rhino now inhabits my world. Pictures and figurines cover the walls and the shelves in my home and office. Early in the morning as I get ready to work out, the baseball cap I don says "Black Rhino" on it. I want its essence to be with me. The imperfect rhino is harmless unless threatened, and then look out: It finishes what it starts and is not fearful of any challenge. It stands its ground. It is one with the earth, surefooted and no nonsense. It is deliberate. It has no wasted motions. It reserves its power until needed.

After the morning session, I took a break. I wrote in my journal, had lunch, and wandered the grounds. I found my way to a big log lying across a stream in a rarely traveled area of the woods. The trees seemed to create a canopy, like a cathedral ceiling, covering the path and log bridge. I walked to the center of the log, held my arms out in a solemn prayer, looked up to nature's cathedral, and sought guidance.

I asked for nature to enter me, to help me see more, to assist me in dealing with the randomness of life, to help me see the larger story, to protect me from getting lost in the smallness of the nonsense of the day. I wanted to find the mountain in me. I wanted to find the sweet spot in life where I could be grateful and appreciative of the very moment, in and of itself, and would understand what that moment meant. I didn't want to take any moment for granted. I asked nature to help me relax into the uncertainty of life, to help me trust my internal knowing. As I prayed, I felt energy surge through my body. I could see colors traveling to and from the tips of my fingers, stretching out to the universe.

More than a month after this shaman experience, I received a letter and picture in the mail. It seems that a person was taking pictures around Esalen that afternoon, saw my stance and praying moment and snapped a picture. She commented that she made a poster of it for her office. I enlarged it too, and it hung in my office as a reminder of my connection to nature and this beautiful shaman world.

After a half hour, I left the bridge and headed back for the afternoon session. There was another world to journey to: the upper world, the home of our spirit teachers and ancestors. The purpose of our upper-world journey was to ask questions that only our spirit teachers could answer. I was told that I had to ask questions that could not be answered with a yes or no. The answer I requested had to require insight and knowledge about an area of existence that I simply did not possess.

Once again the smudge was burning. Once again the drums took me to the heart of the womb. Once again the reality of an alternate world presented itself. This world was entered through an opening in a cloud. The drums again assisted me to enter non-ordinary reality.

So the upper world was entered. As I wandered this non-ordinary reality my spirit teachers approached me. Not surprisingly, I saw both my mom and dad. The three of us had a limited time to communicate because the drumming back in the three-dimensional world where my body was resting was in its later stages already. When it stopped I would have to leave.

I had not thought earlier about what question I would ask, and I did not know the answer. The three of us held hands and I asked, "Where does strength come from?"

The answer I received was clear and calm. "Have compassion for the challenge. Have compassion for the obstacle. Have compassion for the opponent. That is where strength lies. It is only in this way that you can deal with life on your own terms. Only then can you be the master of your life and not the slave to outside emotions or dramas."

It seemed difficult to comprehend that I should have empathy for the challenger. Yet the answer started to resonate with me. In a flash, I got it. Strength comes from letting go of the belief that someone or something can possess me and control my responses to the events of the day. I am part of the mountain, after all. I alone control my thoughts. If I am part of the mountain, than we are all part of it. We are pieces of the whole. If I want strength, I only need to let go of negative feelings, accept the connection, and move toward the light.

We held hands for a moment longer, and then my parents faded into the upper world. I thought I heard singing or a beautiful humming over and above the drumming, but I just don't know. The scene was surreal.

The drumming reached its peak, and then abruptly stopped.

The upper world dissolved.

These shamanic experiences at Esalen got me thinking, not only about challenges to be met in life, but also how best to meet them. For weeks I continued thinking about where fear comes from. Why does darkness trigger a fear response? How can the creative mind overcome darkness and fear? So many people are faced with unbelievable challenges in their lives. They can't ignore them any more than I can ignore mine. We all have to address them as best we can. How creative could the mind be in overcoming problems and meeting danger head on?

CHAPTER 16

The Mulberry Harbors, the Creative Mind, and the Ghost Army

If you want to see the creative mind demonstrated in a real world setting, you really should visit Normandy, France, and the D-Day invasion site on Omaha Beach. Talk about taking hold of the unexpected, living beyond definitions, and being a creative risk taker with everything on the line! When Margie and I went there, I was both surprised and impressed by the ingenuity of the commanders of the Allied Forces, which emerged from them by virtue of necessity.

Before our trip, I had long wanted to go to Normandy. I studied the World War Two invasion in school. I loved reading about this period of history. I never memorized famous dates, but rather was fascinated by the

123

subtle decisions that had changed the course of history. The same types of subtle decisions can change the very course of our lives. I had watched *The Longest Day*. I had seen *Saving Private Ryan*. Nonetheless it was hard to comprehend the magnitude of the effort made across that entire French shoreline until I went there.

When I was asked what I wanted to do to celebrate my sixty-fifth birthday, the decision was easy. Margie and I flew to Paris, then rented a car and headed to Honfleur, France. As we drove from the hotel to the D-Day sites, we saw German bunkers covered with grass. These resembled discarded tombstones. But then we arrived at Omaha Beach. It was as if we were walking on holy ground. There was a stillness that filled the air with each step across the sand. The images of the fierce battle flood your imagination. The German guns are still in place. Inside the stillness I could hear the cries and sense the bravery. I stood there in awe of the courage.

As we walked the beaches of Normandy, I showed my total ignorance when I asked our guide what the concrete objects were, lying just off shore from the sandy beach. The guide looked at me, smiled, and said, "Well, those were probably one of the best kept secrets of World War Two . . . and I guess they're still a secret to some." After we all laughed, we sat down on the benches just across the street from a row of tourist shops in the town of Arromanches and our guide told us the fascinating story of the Mulberry harbors, a system of artificial jetties and roads the Allies had built that floated just off the coastline. Because there wasn't a natural harbor and the water was too shallow for supply ships to come in, they needed to manufacture a structure that would enable them to get supplies to the shore from ships docked in deeper waters.

The Allies needed to figure out how to get

into Fortress Europe. Failure was not an option. The question posed to the Allied Forces was how to invade Europe in order to challenge and defeat the German war machine. It was the time of howling wolves day and night. The Germans had made it nearly impossible to capture a port on the French coast across the English Channel.

But without a port, how would they sustain an invasion? How would the supplies come ashore? They needed a steady shipment of support services, food, tanks, and other armored equipment to sustain the war effort.

Fear can be overcome with the creative mind and a strong belief in the possibility of the impossible. Any challenge can be overcome when the "why not?" starts filtering through your mind, as opposed to the "cannot." I guess after years of seeing signs reading "Stop," "Yield," "Keep off the Grass," "Don't Walk," and "Wrong Way" we get in the habit of restricting our actions so as not to have accidents or get a ticket for even a minor infraction of the law. But then our caution or our anxiety about facing consequences bleeds into our approach to so many other things we would have otherwise normally tried. Caution limits our choices. Safety negates possibility. Fear defeats the possible. Success is often sabotaged merely by entertaining the idea of failure.

After a time, we start equating losing with being a loser. Though there could be nothing further from the truth, this belief leads us into playing it too safe. Our desire never to have to consider losing gets in the way of experiencing otherwise impossible victories.

These were some of the thoughts that entered my mind as we listened to our guide and learned about the Mulberry harbors.

The real challenge was how the Allies would make possible the impossible. How would they overcome fear when there appeared to be no apparatus that even provided a glimmer of hope for success?

Without hope, there is despair. There is a sense of futility. At that point, you either sink into a bottomless pit of no way out or challenge yourself to find your inner hero. Instinct, intuition, and the rightness of the cause must kick in. Then the creative mind can overcome and defeat fear.

The task was monumental. Create a harbor and bring it with you as you cross the English Channel. The risk was defeat or victory for the free world. As teams of experts came together to begin the complex process of devising a manmade harbor, Winston Churchill said: "They must float up and down with the tide. The anchor problem must be mastered. . . . Let me have the best solution worked out. Don't argue the matter. The difficulties will argue for themselves."

What a statement: *The difficulties will argue for themselves.*

And a solution was created. The British engineers and other teams of experts developed and figured out how to build a harbor and transport it across an open sea in time of battle.

At some point in our lives, I know that we all have been faced with a problem that was believed by others to be without a solution. Yet a solution had to be found. If we succeeded, it was done by thinking outside the box, testing the very limits of our creativity, letting our minds run free in seeking an answer, and most of all, by ignoring the critics. In other words, we had to focus, commit, and dedicate ourselves to the solution in order to overcome our fear of failure.

D-Day was June 6, 1944. The harbors were operating by June 18. It only took twelve days.

This book is not a history of the Mulberry harbors, so let us rather consider them as a metaphor of how we might face our own hours of the wolf. How do we overcome crisis? It is not by ignoring reality. We know the blue sky is the blue sky. Rather, it is by creatively evaluating reality, seeing what can't be seen by others, and succeeding where others assure us of failure. For me, it is always done by looking between the lines. When I listen to a song, I always listen to the background music, the subtle chord shifts that make the song so memorable. The background of a story or the subtle change in shade of color in a painting is always the driving force for me.

Life is made up of the subtle. The slight movements. There are so many back stories that make up the total story of history that are ignored. The creation of the Mulberry harbors is an amazing back story to history that tipped the scales toward victory in Europe.

Another back story to accomplishing this great invasion and assisting in the overall war effort is the story of the ghost army. At the same time the D-Day invasion was being planned, the United States ghost army went to work. Known as the Twenty-third Headquarters Special Troops, this unit had the job of impersonating other U.S. Army units in order to fool the Germans about how large the Allied Forces were and where they were stationed. They used fake tanks, sound trucks, and other theatrical devices to trick the enemy. Sound foolish? Seem outlandish? Yet, without even trying, nothing can be started. How audacious a scheme!

The Allies' leaders were facing a world-changing challenge. Each day was filled with mind-numbing decisions that had to be made. Each decision was critical. Waging a war to stop the Nazis took hold of their imaginations. There were many great leaders in this effort. Let's look at three. Three men who by today's standards would very likely either be considered "over the hill" or passed over for promotion in order to give younger, fresher-faced up-and-comers an opportunity.

Winston Churchill. Born in 1874, he died in 1965 at the age of ninety-one. During the creative, stressful, momentous times of the Mulberry harbors, he was already seventy years old. Let's stop right there. Seventy. A number. Remember, the number is not the man. The number does not eliminate imagination. It is only by living through great successes and tragic failures, such as the failure Churchill faced at the Battle of Gallipoli in Turkey in World War One, that we gain a wealth of knowledge that then permits us to analyze and put in context what is before us.

Dwight D. Eisenhower, the commander of the Allied invasion, its operation overlord, was born in 1890 and died in 1969. He was fifty-four when he directed the Normandy landing and took the Allied Forces to victory. The complications were not to be believed. Even on the fateful day of decision when the weather was a critical factor and one voice had to be heard to say, "Go," it was the voice of this warrior that was heard. Later, he was elected President of the United States because of his heroic leadership on momentous occasions such as D-Day. People wanted to believe that anything was possible. He gave them the vision of making the impossible possible. If he could lead an army to conquer an enemy led by a man that many had labeled the devil incarnate, they could overcome their daily dragons. This statesman stepped forward and led more than an army to victory.

Our third hero was Franklin D. Roosevelt. He was born in 1882 and died in 1945. At the time of the military campaign to free Europe, he was sixty-two years old. Though not in his dot-age, today he would be eligible to receive early retirement. This inspiring man led a nation through the Depression, then Pearl Harbor, and onwards to victory in Europe. He led a nation to believe in itself, saying, "The only thing we have to fear is fear itself."

Age did not hold back any of these great men. The day of decision was presented to them and they acted with honor, dignity, wisdom, and courage. On the day of decision, they were ageless. They made a choice of how to respond to life—and choices do not ask how old we are.

So these leaders, together enacting a grand design to defeat a monster, were between the ages of fifty-four and seventy. Yet in our day and age, those within the same span of ages are often treated or treat themselves as if they have lost a step. Hiring practices discriminate against workers over fifty. Companies frequently replace mature workers who hold key positions simply because of the year recorded on their birth certificates. Barring illness and frailty, however, elders in our society have the wisdom, history, skill, and life experience to meet any challenge of any day.

What false belief of inadequacy due to some arbitrary birthday prevents the rest of us from leading ourselves to freedom like our World War Two heroes led the world? Think about it. When did age start becoming a litmus test for our ability to start, finish, or accomplish anything? When did we start using it to impose limitations on ourselves?

Creative. Brave. Honorable. Fearless. Courageous. Smart. Hopeful. Noble. What age would you place next to any of these words? None.

The wolf may approach heroes at midnight, but heroes like Churchill, Eisenhower, and Roosevelt, conquer their fear—or act in spite of it. So what can we learn from them? One lesson is to see each moment as the first and last one. Another is to exert ourselves completely each day, or as many athletes say, "Leave it all on the field." These

129

three leaders left it all on the field.

Don't we want to be used up at the very end? We don't really need any gas left in the tank when our journey is done, so what are we saving it for? Why are we holding back? I ask again: What is the worth of a single day lived as 100 percent you being 100 percent present?

I decided to continue my investigations while in France, this time at the French Alps on an ice field in Chamonix. Another mountain. Another timeless moment. Another day filled with effort, exhaustion, and accomplishment. After a brief stop to visit friends in Geneva, dinner in Yvoire, France, and a drive through Megeve, we found ourselves at the base of Mont Blanc. The goal, the next challenge awaiting Margie and me, was to cross the famous ice fields.

CHAPTER 17

The Ice Field
and the Lesson

Something about Mont Blanc has always captured my imagination. Situated in the part of the Alps located between France and Italy, it is the highest mountain in Western Europe. To locals, it is known as either *La Dame Blanche* (French for "The white lady") or *Il Bianco* (Italian for "The white one"), depending on which side of the border you are on. After Margie and I returned from the Himalayas, the mystique of mountains still drew us in. We approached the snowcapped glacial mountain from the French side, making a visit to Chamonix.

Almost every type of outdoor winter sport can be found in Chamonix. But two adventures in particular were waiting for us there. One was crossing the ice fields of the glacier, and the other was paragliding off the cliffs surrounding Chamonix. To cross the ice fields, we took the Montenvers rack railway up Mont Blanc and exited at the bottom of its glacial peak. At that point we made our way through an ice cave. This set the tone for the terrain that lay ahead. On the other side of the cave, we rented gear needed to cross the ice fields and hired a guide. We saw no signs that barred trekkers because of age. So Margie and I decided to go for it. We put on our crampons, had safety ropes tied around our waists and were handed ice axes. Our guide took a photograph of us as we stepped onto the ice field. In this picture, I'm looking forward and Margie is looking to the side. What you can't tell is what she's saying to me, which is, "Last time, Lipton." We began to appreciate that this was not a typical hike through a mountain range.

Full commitment and strenuous effort would be needed to traverse the ice field. Once begun there would be no turning back. There was no cab to call after an hour or so. The steep terrain, the ice, the snow, the crevasses that needed to be dealt with (the reason for the ropes) and knowing that there would be no exit until we reached the other side gave us a pure adrenaline rush and set our imaginations racing. We had to commit to the effort.

The commitment to the day had to be made.

The word "commitment" struck a chord with me out there in the ice field. Do we commit to the day completely, each day, or do we phone it in? Commitment to the days of my life became my mantra on Mont Blanc.

After hours of maneuvering the crevasses with the help of our trusty guide, we made it to Italy, got off the mountain, and then found our way back to France for a well-deserved glass of wine, some French bread, and a wonderful assortment of cheeses. As we sat around later that evening in Megeve, I wondered why. Why had we made our effort? What was the purpose of it? What was accomplished? Again a mountain and a meaning. Again a day and an adventure. Again a challenge to the mind, spirit, and body with every step.

The meaning for me came back to the idea

of an ageless day. It hit me suddenly that our days are only limited by us. That it is so typical to look at a watch and say, for instance, "It is time to take a break or eat," whether or not we need a break or feel hungry. We are like Pavlov's dogs. We've been trained to respond to our timekeeping contraptions, as opposed to tuning in to how we feel at any particular moment and responding to what we sense.

I looked at the clock ticking in the corner of the hotel restaurant. What have we done? We invented the clock. The clock was not there before humankind. And we invented the calendar. We started the celebration of birthdays. Before that everything was simply nature at work: the sunrise, the sunset, living without counting minutes or hours or days. It just was the day . . . light or dark.

Then we came along and for some reason needed to establish boundaries around activities. With boundaries came categories. With categories came signs and boxes. We invented timekeeping and began living by the tool we invented as if it had a power greater than the simple purpose we gave to it of timekeeping. Today time is almost a type of religion. Massive clocks are in the square. The church bells ring at prescribed moments. We have, to a great extent, become prisoners of time. Worse, we have permitted time to change how we see ourselves. We see ourselves as young or old, as capable or incapable of doing the things we dream of doing, not measured by our desires or abilities, but by the arbitrary ticking of time.

The invention of timekeeping has stolen from us the simple joy of the passing clouds, afternoon rains, and beautiful suns setting just over the horizon. With that theft, has come the treatment of days as if they were commodities. Businesses buy and sell "time": advertising minutes. We can also hire people by the hour. Some businesses, like

133

the law, require time to be managed—and paid for—in six-minute intervals. An hour is considered ten sections. An hour is not even an hour anymore to those practicing certain professions: Therapists nonsensically offer fifty-minute "hours."

Did you ever notice that no other animal keeps time? All other creatures let nature be their guide. Perhaps we could learn from their example.

The majesty of nature is very compelling. Humankind can invent the greatest inventions. We can send a spacecraft to Mars (and when the images are shown on the evening news we'll watch if it doesn't conflict with our favorite sitcom), yet it won't stop us in our tracks like the sun setting behind a mountain range or seeing the sun's rays glistening on the ocean surface.

Wanting to find out what Mount Blanc looked like from the sky, the next morning I hired another guide who took me to the top of one of the cliffs in Chamonix. He only spoke French. I did not. He only said two words as we reached the cliff's ledge, "Run. Jump." As I ran and jumped, I thought, *What the heck am I doing?* For a second, suspended in the air, my legs kept running, like some cartoon character about to drop. That was a real commitment.

I paraglided over the village. Margie slept in. As I glided through the skies, I couldn't help wondering why I wasn't using every day of my life to live in the moment and jump with such total commitment into the arms of my destiny.

That night, I slept like a rock. The wolf does not intrude on full days of living. It only haunts the mind when we know we have cheated ourselves out of a day.

In retrospect, I can see that the mountain was our teacher. In studying it, we better understood ourselves. One of the lessons of Mont Blanc was pushing through exhaustion. We knew there would be plenty of time to rest when we got home. Whether it is crossing an ice field or enjoying gardening on a bright spring day at home, find that piece of you that is calling out for attention and nurturing. Any such day is then a day of adventure. We can start all over again every time we open our eyes. Yes, we might get hurt. But what is the cost of living safe? That is no life. A balance must be found between our daily routines and our extraordinary efforts. There has to be a way to live a life that matters. There has to be a way to live a day that counts. We have to learn to build mountain-like experiences in other settings, such as I do when I'm riding on a motorcycle.

135

CHAPTER 18

The Death and the Birth of the Warrior

An old friend of mine always challenged the fashion police and was totally irreverent. Rules that others complied with, he found humorous at best. Steve drove cars too fast, believing traffic rules and speed limits were merely suggestions. Although I didn't approve of this behavior and tried to have him see the danger in it, he would slip back into this behavior periodically. Maybe it was being the child of Nazi concentration camp survivors that made him rebel about any rules or directives.

One truth I've learned over the years is that people who live through major upheavals or whose family members have lived through crisis either put the regular ups and downs of life in context and relax into the day or they are crushed by the slightest breeze. My friend was not crushed. He just found life a bit absurd. The tragedy that his parents had lived through put a spin on life that made him conclude rules were nonsense. In fact, he believed he couldn't trust people who tried to impose rules. The more rules, the less trustworthy they were in his eyes.

Basically, Steve saw the way life generally worked as one really big Rube Goldberg puzzle, some complex cartoon contraption that does a simple common task, like a room full of levers, slides, bells, whistles, and balls going down chutes and through tunnels to end up having the last of a dozen balls hit a peg that flushes a toilet. He didn't see why it all had to be so complicated when all anyone has to do is just be direct, honest, and not take anything too seriously. Steve also was a big believer in Occam's razor, the principle of looking for the simplest, least complex answer to any question.

Although rules meant nothing to him, if my friend gave me his word, then without a shred of doubt I knew he would stand by it. I was lucky to have such a friend, especially during my most challenging of times. Steve had the gift of putting my obstacles in context. He was smart, witty, loud, and there for a friend in a heartbeat. I appreciated that he was genuine, as authenticity is a hard quality to find these days. I also appreciated that he was able to see that there is some basic absurdity to our whole human experiment.

When we stop and think, we must admit he was right: It is humorous. Steve compared human behavior to a huge anthill with all the ants scurrying here and there, being industrious in their efforts, serious beyond description, but ants never the less. Steve always felt that someone or something was playing a big gag on us. It was one joke and only a few were in on it. The rest had bought in to the illusion and never quite figured out that there is no reason not to enjoy the ride. He figured that since the only exit from this trip is the final exit, why should we not live large and loud. Small and quiet never cut it in his world.

Did he offend some people? Absolutely. Did he make others cringe? Indeed. But he spoke the truth of what he believed and railed against the political correctness that so often drowned out people's logic and sincerity.

When Steve got ill, it caught us all by surprise. The cancer swept through him like a raging forest fire. From not feeling well, to aches and pains, to diagnosis, to chemo, to hair loss and wigs, to weight loss, to the last movie, phone call, and comment, his dying taught me many lessons. Here was another larger-than-life person I cared about who died in his early fifties, just like my mom and dad. Within six months he was gone.

His cancer was so swift in its destructive path that it shook us to our very core. From tall and strapping, to bent over and frail, cancer attacked him brutally and altered his body. Yet, through it all, he would joke. When he lost his hair, he got a bad wig and wore it knowing exactly how it looked—and tipped it like a top hat.

Near the end he became gentler in his observations. He wanted to hear the good things happening for others in the day. But when we told him about those good moments, unlike some who feign attention, he was focused and totally present. I could see the joy in his eyes when he heard good news. Each minute became a critical time left to look at a friend. Touch a hand. Drink a glass of cold water. Just to sip water, catch a piece of an ice cube in his mouth and crunch down on it made him laugh. Simple became profound. We talked about following your bliss, letting go of grudges, laughing with abandon, crying without shame.

The last movie we went to see together was *The Matrix*. It seemed to make sense at such a time. Is life just a grand mind trip and nothing more? During the movie, he got up and said he was going to the men's room. After about ten minutes I walked out to the lobby to find him. He was sitting on a bench alone. His head was down. I sat next to him and held his hand. He said he was weary and asked if it was it all right to go home. He just couldn't make it through the whole movie. I helped him to the car and as we drove home I knew that this was our last drive together.

Ever think about that? What the last of anything would be? The last kiss. The last hug. The last glass of cold water. The last good cry. The last time waking up next to your lover. Since each time we do anything it could be the last time, what should that single moment, that single day, mean to us?

We left about halfway through that movie, as he was suffering too much. To this day, I still haven't seen it to its end. Two weeks later he was gone.

About a week before the final hospital visit, he called me. I knew time was short. The conversation was direct and to the point. He said, "Paul, in the end it is just about being a good friend. Being there." He hung up. A few days later we were all standing around his bed at the hospital. It was the deathwatch. He was unconscious. We told stories and hoped he heard us. We told him he was a good friend, and to rest. From some place that I don't know, he suddenly drew strength. He sat up in bed, opened his eyes, stared at his wife and daughter, Margie and me, and simply said, "Thank you." Then he lay back down, closed his eyes, and left.

There is not a day that goes by that I don't think of Steve. Literally, I think of him every day. It makes me smile. He understood the meaning of a day. When I think about him I remember his favorite sayings. Steve had a few great lines. When someone would be upset with him for his raw honesty, for instance, he would say,

"Have them take a ticket and get at the end of the complaint line." Another was, "Fuck 'em if they can't take a joke." He never meant this in a dark

way. It was always said lightly and with a quizzical look, as if to ask, "You aren't taking any of this seriously, are you?"

When I see people taking themselves too seriously or trying too hard to make some point, I think back to Steve. When I hear people explain how complex a problem is, I think of Occam's razor. I smile and move on.

What is immortality? Being remembered. Living 100 percent present as 100 percent you. Understanding the inside joke, and going with it anyway. Not holding back. Not compromising. Risking. Challenging ourselves. Laughing at our flaws. Enjoying the ride.

Which takes me to the ride.

Steve and I always talked about our love of motorcycles. Neither of us rode one, but it was frequently the topic of conversation. We would drop by motorcycle stores and look, smell, touch, and sit on them and talk about the adventures we could have. The main discussion always surrounded Steve McQueen and his love of bikes, and the jump he made famous in the movie *The Great Escape.* The chase, the barbed wire fence, the freedom on one side, and the war camp on the other. The liberation or the confinement.

The jump always triggered in us the knowing that freedom is within our grasp. Time, responsibilities, work, fear of injury, and a false sense of the limitations of age seemed to get in the way of acting on our desire to ride. We talked about being too old to start such a young person's sport. Reflexes, sitting positions, and weather conditions take their toll on anyone who rides, and this toll appeared too much for us to handle. So we voluntarily put ourselves in the box of "can't at our age."

It was probably a month after Steve's funeral that I found myself back in the motorcycle store. My fingers ran over a black Honda Magna. I signed up for the safety course, took the test, and failed. When I flunked that driving test, I thought that the universe was trying to tell me something: Clearly my reflexes were not sharp enough. I went home reconciled to the fact that my dream was not to be. But that night I kept thinking about failure and success and the narrow razor's edge that separates one from the other. In the morning I called the driving school and asked for permission to take the driving test again. The next week I took it and passed.

A few weeks later the Magna was in the driveway. A year later the Magna was traded in for a Kawasaki Vulcan. The power went from a 750-cubic centimeter engine to a 1,500-c.c. machine. Then it happened. I saw the Yamaha Midnight Warrior, a 1,700-c.c. hotrod. I remember the comment I made to Margie before I bought it, "My choice is either a walker or a Warrior." I went for the risk. I have never cared for walkers.

I had the Chinese symbol for "warrior" painted on the tank and rode her whenever I could. She challenged me to risk and let go, to just be in the moment, unconnected to any phone, radio, fax, or obligation, to be one with her. Although I rode her too many times too fast, going over 100 M.P.H., I never felt in danger. I lovingly called her "the beast." A day on the Beast became an adventure of back roads and out of the way bars patronized by truckers and locals in pickups drinking beer and playing pool. The Everglades. The Florida Keys. The mountains of North Carolina. I went to out-of-the-way destinations just to take her to them. I commented that she decided where we would go . . . not me.

Meeting up with soon to be new friends and sharing biker stories, of close calls, bad weather, sights seen, and the latest mo-torcycle gear or gadgets, I learned that there are two types of bikers: those who drop the bike and walk away from it, and those who drop the bike and don't walk away from it. The common denominator is that sooner or later everyone drops the bike and risks the fall.

Although I didn't completely understand how the fall happened, it happened. Was it the gravel? The back wheel spinning out? Just a freaky move? Whatever it was, I went down with the Beast on top of me. My helmet hit the pavement and cracked. My gloves braced the fall somewhat, but the damage was done. My shoulder separated and the hot engine burned my leg.

At sixty-six, after over ten years of riding, that was probably not the best of places to find myself. But there I was. I was dazed. I wiggled my way out from under the bike. I was shaking. My left shoulder seemed not to be where it should be.

But this story is not about falling. This is about getting back up. The type three shoulder separation was going to heal. The burn was not bad. My cracked helmet saved me from a cracked head. The lesson? Sometimes you just have to be lucky when you hit an unlucky moment in life. We all hit times when everything goes wrong. If in such moments we look deep inside and see how it could have been worse, we can be grateful for small gifts. We can get back up and move on.

After emergency rooms and X-rays, the course of my recovery was set.

As I wore the sling the doctor gave me, I started hearing the comments. "You are too old for motorcycles," "You sure learned your lesson," "What were you trying to prove?"

I am sure you've heard such comments before, judgments offered after the fact, questioning our choices. They seem designed to put us back in line. But if we believe that the day is to be lived fully, such comments don't linger.

My doctor was taking follow-up X-rays and doing one of the last examinations of my shoulder about three months after the fall. As I was buttoning up my shirt, he asked me if I was planning to get back on the Beast. "Of course," I said. He smiled and said he was hoping I would say that. "Enjoy it all. I mean, Paul, why not?"

Why not, indeed! Steve would not have wanted it any other way. He would have looked at me and asked, "What exactly are you waiting for, some fancy invitation? The bike is lonely. Ride!"

Now back to the other Steve, Steve McQueen. One of his bikes was the Triumph Bonneville. I had seen a red and white one. It was a 900-c.c. 2006 Triumph Scrambler, a retro of a 1960's model. Something about McQueen's jump to freedom in *The Great Escape* caused me to buy this sweet machine. Was the jump my metaphor for life? To risk. Escape the routine. Jump past the confinement and limitations we place ourselves in. Whatever my reason was for buying it, it is the Triumph Scrambler that I mainly ride now. I did add three words in bold red to the bike tank: The Great Escape. Every time I get on it, I feel lighter and looser.

Today, the Great Escape has a riding companion. Margie, as a gift to me, got her own motorcycle license, after passing her safety course test on her first attempt, and she now rides an 883-c.c. Harley Davidson Iron Sportster. At the age of sixty-five, wearing an Icon Moto motorcycle jacket, she saddles up and rides fearlessly.

After a Saturday or Sunday morning ride to some restaurant, I still enjoy bringing the motorcycles to rest, putting down the kickstand, taking off our helmets, and having some passerby say, "Good for you." I always think about those comments and realize they say more about the passersby than us. We are just living a single day for everything it can be.

My accident got me thinking about choices people make. There are no rules or regulations that

144

float "out there" being superimposed on any of us. The only rules or regulations that exist are self-imposed rules. That being the case, what we do in life comes down to our definitions of ourselves. When the moment arrives to make a choice, what choice do we make? Do we push ourselves or step back and limit our options?

CHAPTER 19

The Five Decisions

Since each day matters and since we make hundreds of decisions every day—small and large—we need to be conscious of how we decide. These decisions could very well change our lives, or the lives our family members, for better or worse. Looking back at my own life, I can see that five major decisions sent me down an entirely different road than I originally envisioned. I also see that I do not control too much of anything. Everyone else is also making decisions, seizing opportunities, or letting opportunities slip by, so the results of my decisions seem to have arrived through twists and turns like playing with a Rubik's cube. As I choose and as I intersect with others, the possible permutations of consequences are truly mindboggling.

As I sit here writing, I am reflecting about how I went to Colorado to see my family on a specific date in July, and all that went into making that possible. I am reflecting on the details of my day today: whom I met and when I met them, whom I missed meeting by a hair of a second. It seems that the randomness of life meets an individual's choice at every turn.

Think that a single decision is not critical? Then

consider how long we typically take to make major decisions that can send our lives in a different direction. Did the choice take a second? Less? A minute or two? After Robert Kennedy gave his acceptance speech after the California primary, one of his campaign aides decides to escort him through the kitchen instead of the hotel ballroom front door. A parade route is decided on after President John Kennedy chooses to go to Dallas to mend political fences. Both men lost their lives due to those routine types of decisions. Their lives and the world changed forever.

For myself, I decided to go to law school at Washington University in St. Louis instead of accept an assistantship in political science offered me by Penn State University. Years later, as I sit here in a coffee shop in Colorado as opposed to one in some other city, I can think back about these and similar choices that ultimately, somehow, led me here. Whereas someone else through his or her choices is now living in Dallas instead of Chicago or works as a salesman instead of a doctor, a painter, or a . . . fill in the blank. A choice. A decision. Who did we spend our lives with? Did we have children? How did they turn out? How did it change us forever? What decision was the tipping point that we could never step back from?

Some choices are like turning a corner—and maybe it is a corner where we choose not to decide, and thus, when our lives change, we end up believing it was out of our control. Whether we acted or failed to act, it was a decision. Many choices are irreversible. Some put us on a dirt road in an open field with options all around us, while others put us on a track that lies in the path of a speeding freight train. We encounter "corners" hundreds of times a day.

The first time I remember thinking about such corners was when I was reading Thornton

Wilder's play *Our Town* as a young boy. This is the story of one person's journey back from death to observe a single day in her life in Grover's Corner. It is Emily's twelfth birthday. Each minute of that twenty-four-hour day, despite its ordinariness, is meaningful in hindsight. I know how meaningful, for, like Emily, looking back on it now, I can still hear the tick-tock sound of the clock that my dad made as he read "The Legend of Sleepy Hollow" aloud to me. Time keeps marching and winding our lives down. Thinking about it now, there is a certain sense of frailty to that moment. I get a wistful feeling.

The questions hanging over the story of *Our Town* are finally asked. Why don't people appreciate the gift of a single day? Does anyone pause to recognize the finite nature of a day and a life? Why does everyone act as if life will last forever? Sooner or later we all have the lookback. Grover's Corner is a destination that we all reach if we live long enough and have any shred of self-awareness. The message that *Our Town* holds for us is that it is not only the single day that is so vital; every small comment, gesture, and intention also matters, because each has consequences.

During our very limited time on Earth, we make decisions about how we will live. Although we may have very little to say about the quantity of days allotted to us, we do have a say about the quality of each day.

But quality is subjective. How to measure it? How to calibrate it? It is tied so tightly to our preferences and choices.

So I come back to the five decisions. Five seems to me like the perfect number. Four would be shy of the full story. A list of six could just as easily become seven or eight. Five has a rhythm and pulse to it. Maybe it has something to do with the five senses: the five decisions that defined my lifetime. What brought me from there to here? What remarkable decisions changed it all? The decisions fall into the following five categories: health, family and friends, spirit, learning, and fun.

Did I perhaps on occasion decide to let someone else direct my life's trajectory in any of these categories? If so, is that why the midnight mind sometimes haunts me, telling me to fear that my story will never be told once I am not here to tell it? So I ask: What is the worth of a single decision? Was it the wolf that caused me to choose out of fear? Is it age that limits what I think I can still do? Should any of us ever let age factor into pursuing a dream that could still be fulfilled? Aren't we forever in the grand design of creating our lives?

If it comes down to five decisions in the journey of striving to be a hero in a world that seems anything but heroic, what causes someone to go one way or another? Consider the choices made regarding the D-Day invasion, such as, "Should we wait until the weather clears over the English Channel or go despite imperfect conditions?" What causes anyone either to risk it all and let the chips fall where they may or to pull back? When does the fear of failure give way to acting out of a belief that failure is acceptable if the effort is fully made to succeed?

Is It Ever Too Late to Make a Decision to Change?

I completely understand that I am older. I am not delusional that I am still eighteen or thirty or anything other than the age that matches the years I have been alive. But those years, other than the experiences they gave me, do not have to define who I am or the nature of the constantly unfolding journey I am on. Too many of my friends engage in self-limitation simply because they have hit a date marker that seems arbitrary to me. I recently heard someone say that he divided life into three sections: young . . . till about thirty-five. Then middle . . . till about sixty-seven. Then old . . . after sixty-seven. He was in the "after sixty-seven" bracket. All arbitrary numbers, but fairly commonly chosen age markers in any discussion of age. Listening to this, I found it interesting that a bright person would divide up his life by numbers as opposed to lived experiences, no matter the number.

I pointed out that there was still time to reengage in the adventure of his life and not only concentrate on what some calendar or birthday supposedly signified. He could make a different decision now, and our decisions count. In reply, he said he felt it was too late and he had no desire to even try.

How do we define wealth? What is valuable? For each of us, the answer is different. For each of us, one road may be more important and attractive than another. This leads us to make certain decisions and thus, at least in part, to live the lives we live. Just as the characters in *The Razor's Edge* made different decisions and took dramatically different paths, so can we. Nonetheless, I feel I have to ask, where does our destiny lie? As we get ready to jump into life, at any stage or age, which is the destiny that will open up for us? We may be surprised. Each of the five major decisions we make has the potential to take us down a whole new path.

We don't need to accept that we can become too old to shift gears. We don't need to start with some worn-out idea that time has slipped away. The creation of the day forever awaits our artistry. We may feel locked into a specific path by circumstances beyond our control, but we can still dream and in some small way find our personal sanctuary of peace and fulfillment. Change comes from within. We can listen to our inner voice, which speaks for an invisible

151

part of us that wants to be recognized. No effort is too small. No change is too insignificant. The slightest adjustments can create major changes in our lives, if we, at least, begin.

A theory known as the butterfly effect illustrates this concept. The idea is that some small event, such as the flap of a butterfly's wings, amplified over time and distance, would be sufficient to cause major changes, such as a tornado in another part of the world.

It's similar to what happens after tossing a stone in a lake. It ripples the water and some child's toy boat starts bouncing around. Such is life. At any age, we can begin again by making a small change. But that requires a decision to act.

Getting up a half hour earlier than usual to take a walk as the sun rises could change the state of our health. Instead of racing through that walk, walking around the neighborhood, listening to the birds chirping, and watching the community wake up can be a moment of meditation that colors our outlook for the entire day. As we walk, our focus changes. Colors seem brighter. Sounds seem sharper.

For me, music sets the tone for the day. I immerse myself in life, then make the first cup of coffee, put on my favorite song, and begin. I take my journal off the shelf and make a few notes. One note made is an affirmation of how I want to live that day. Over the years since I began this practice, I have seen a pattern of certain repeating phrases. Those words, like silent prayers, are: "Be grateful," "Live in a state of grace," "Appreciate the blessing of the day," and "Respect the moment for the gift that it is." Over time that journal has been converted into a blog that I post online.

How would a slight change of how you spend even a half hour start to affect your life? How different would your world be if you just stopped and refocused for a minute? Could you break an old pattern? If you can, then your destiny is still being written. Your future is boundless. Whatever the decision may be for you, consider that it is a way of shifting the direction of your life, moving away from some previously ordained destination to somewhere new.

The five decisions I have identified are really five categories of consideration. A decision made in each of these categories became a tipping point in my life and could be in your life, too. It's common to wonder what went right or wrong in a life: for instance, why do some married people have loving relationships while others constantly fight with spouses they once deeply loved? There was a decision made at some point, wasn't there, setting the direction of these relationships for better or worse?

Decision #1: Health

Are we physically challenging ourselves? Are we prioritizing ourselves in our days? Or do we never seem to make time for ourselves? Do we do too many errands or have a to-do list that does not include us on it? For some reason, in a whole week of twenty-four-hour days, there is often no space found for a few hours just to take care of ourselves. The excuses are many. One is that we are too tired. Another is that it requires too much effort. The big one is that we are too busy. The too busy excuse is the usual one I hear. It is as if we are too important and too needed by others to be important or needed by ourselves. When I hear this, I am frankly amazed.

Recently, I heard someone say that he couldn't have his heart and arteries checked because he couldn't find the time. Really? He looked pale, was overweight, smoked, and had all the signs of a ticking time bomb

153

in his chest, yet he decided he was too busy to visit the doctor. He had appointments on his calendar and none included his health.

What is important in life? If not your physical and mental well-being, then what exactly? I heard a friend comment that he could not break out of his depression. He had reached the heights of monetary success with a mansion, a yacht, and the most expensive of cars and artwork. So I asked, "What is causing this distress?"

My friend looked at me and said, "Life is spinning away too fast. I can buy anything I want except time. I can't turn the clock back. I can't return to the past. My life is just slipping away. I'm upset by the uncontrollable passing of days." He also said that he never took the time to take care of his health. He had made the decisions years earlier that exercise was not financially productive. He hadn't seen the benefit in making the time necessary to work out since it took him away from making money. He had now long passed the tipping point with his health.

There will come a moment when the road back to health is blocked. The heart attack. The stroke. The diabetes. The no energy for the kids or grandkids. What has value? Health.

We can decide to start doing what is necessary to be healthier at any age. We can begin caring for ourselves at any time, even if we haven't done so in the past. Although I have heard others say it is too late to start, it is really only too late if the day is looked at like some straightjacket.

For me, my decision to be healthy in recent years has meant doing CrossFit training. When I initially read about CrossFit I decided it was probably too extreme. The regimen involves do-ing a specified "Workout of the Day," or WOD, that is quite demanding. I doubted I could do it without collapsing. But I also knew that if I didn't try I would regret it. The wolf feeds on regrets. No, I decided, I needed—and wanted—to push myself to my personal best each day and not pretend that I was just fine "for my age." Each morning I needed to redefine what I could accomplish physically. It was as important to me, if not more important, than any other activity in the day.

Each day at 6:00 A.M. those of us who do CrossFit get ready for the morning workout. It has now been over two and a half years since I began this regimen and at my last physical my family doctor wanted to know what was going on. My blood pressure was down and every other measure was also better than it had been in years.

The decision was made one day to work at being physically healthy. But that single decision has also changed me mentally and emotionally. I feel more complete. I finally feel that I am respecting my body, the gift God gave me. It is as if I've woken up to the possibility of myself. In joining the CrossFit gym in my community, I felt a rebirth of my spirit.

Exercising doesn't have to be extreme. Just start. Keep the butterfly effect in mind, not the desire for instant gratification. Take it on. You will find the slow, steady return to being healthier feels wonderful.

What choices could you make within the health category? Is it drinking, smoking, or drugs that needs to be addressed? What addiction, of one kind or another, is holding you back or providing the excuse that prevents you from being all you can be? What is your health worth? How valuable is your health to your family? What model are you setting for your kids?

Don't give up on your body. Don't say it is not worth the effort. Demand more from yourself. Set the clock. Get up. The challenge awaits you. Commit to five minutes. Remember what it felt like to be more. Remember what it felt like to care. Start the climb back one step at a time, one flight of stairs at a time. Make it a family project. You are worth it.

Decision #2: Family and Friends

What makes any of us a success? If we think it is only the money we've accumulated or the length of the driveway leading up to our house, then we may feel empty. Unless there are loving people around us, the emptiness catches up with us. The day is only filled with endless possibilities if we can share it with those who matter to us. Has a decision been made to be present in our family's life and our friends' lives?

Being present in the lives of the people closest to us is a decision. We have the choice to get home early enough to tuck our kids in at bedtime. I can recall sitting down at the edge of the bed and watching as my daughter settled under the covers. Then a book was chosen and read. Once it was done, she'd ask for a second story. Even if it was a long day and weariness had set in, it was often the second story that was the sweetest moment. It was her smile and laughter at being allowed to stay up a little longer and listen to her dad's voice, and the feeling of connection between us, that was precious. When I asked my granddaughter what the best part of her day was her answer was the second book read before it was time to go to sleep. She's like her mom was at the same age.

If you have children, has dinnertime been set aside so that television, iPads, and games are not permitted into the family circle? Is there recognition that your home is a sanctuary and not just another company boardroom? Family connections won't stop when your kids move away and have their own kids. Keep those connections alive. The layers in a life just get thicker and richer. Make the effort to be present for your family.

Harry Chapin's classic song "Cat's in the Cradle" is the story of a father and son putting off making time for each other at different ages as the boy grows up and the man grows old. Life is a circle. We end where we began. So along the way we should show commitment, love, and how important we are to each other by spending time together. What else is there?

I believe in making gestures that show my love, such as the one for our older daughter's fortieth birthday. A party was being held in Boulder, Colorado. A few days beforehand, I called my son-in-law and asked where the celebration was being held. After he gave me the name of the restaurant, he asked why I wanted to know. I told him I wanted to send her flowers with a little note as a surprise. The next day Margie and I made the easiest decision we had made in a long time. Instead of sending flowers, we surprised my daughter by flying from Miami to casually walk in on the celebration with the flowers in hand. A decision was made: Be connected no matter the distance. Make the effort.

How often do we travel for tragedy, but not for a party? It has always puzzled me when people drop everything to travel to a funeral when they won't for celebrations. Travel for the party with the living people. My friends asked me how much the trip to Boulder cost. I know it was time away from my work and the airplane tickets were a bit expensive to buy on short notice, but I didn't mind. When Margie and I walked into the birthday party, my daughter was elated. Most of our daughter's friends said that their own parents would not have done the same thing. They thought it was extraordinary. But why? Traveling for the celebration is now a treasured memory. This is the type of thing we do that can make a single day amazing.

When my sister turned seventy, my niece called and said there was to be a surprise party at the Hourglass Tavern in Hell's Kitchen in New York City. Seventy is a major milestone. I can remember my sister's Sweet Sixteen birthday, her senior prom, and so many adventures we had together as kids growing up on Long Island. With our parents gone, it is just the two of us. Only we are left to remember the small house in North Bellmore where we grew up, the family cookouts on Sundays, and life in the '50s and '60s before I went off to college and law school. The morning of her birthday, we flew up from Miami, and that night we sauntered into the party. The look on my sister's face was priceless. It was the ultimate gift. I even brought a Sweet Sixteen party tiara for her to wear. She wore it with pride. We laughed and cried.

What is your time worth? What has value? Before the party, Margie and I went down to Ground Zero. We had not been there since 9/11. As we sat, meditated, and talked about the tragedy, I thought about the fathers, mothers, children, and friends who were lost there, and how all of them, the ones lost and the surviving family members, would give anything for one single day together one more time. One more hug. One more family dinner. One more second story as they tucked their kids into bed. One more knowing nudge to a friend about some long ago memory. One more moment. One more look back at the ones who matter. What matters? What makes the day make sense? So much of life is just empty chatter and gossip. So much of it is hurtful and painful. So often the ego gets in the way of the simple "I'm sorry." If we can't breathe with our family and friends who can we breathe with?

I made a conscious decision to be part of my fami-

158

ly's life. It wasn't always that way. Fortunately, the world woke me up to let me know that the connection was dying. Just being there is so appreciated. Being present on a day of joy is unmatchable. So I recommend that you make the effort to be present to the ones who matter to you. Connect with something bigger.

I learned the lesson that I am a critical member of my family. I used to think that it was "me and my family." I felt it was my job to provide for them and I saw them as separate from me. Home was a place I went, like work, to take care of the bills and other responsibilities. But then I went to Esalen on a retreat. Our group was talking about what giving feels like. The facilitator asked me to draw a circle and list all the members of my family. When I listed my wife and daughters only, he asked me, "Where are you?"

I said, "That *is* my family." Until then I hadn't realized that my perception made me an outsider to my family. I suddenly felt the distance between their day and mine.

He smiled and asked again, "Where are you? You must be in the circle, too. You must take care of your whole family, and that includes you."

After that I made a decision and became one with my family. Now when I am getting ready for an important business meeting, I always remember that only with a strong family am I fully prepared to be my best.

After a lecture I presented at an industry retreat, I was once asked, "What makes up a winning team in any critical business proposal?" They wanted to know how to best staff the team. I said, "You start with your family." I got a few stares, and then a few knowing nods. I said, "It all starts with a strong family because that is your moral support. Your family is your back bench that provides you the sanctuary needed to be all you can be in any business moment."

What is a winning team? It begins at home. It begins by being in a loving, caring relationship, and then spreads out from there. We can never be fully successful in any venture without the home team. The home-court advantage is an invisible power behind any effort.

Decision #3: Spirit

We have to believe that there is the larger story to be told. Can we accept that we are part of the mountain, part of a bigger, bolder story? Have we made a decision to connect to more than the daily events and gossip of the day? Making a spiritual decision can change our lives.

When I was a young boy, my dad took me outside as the sun was setting. I had been upset about something that happened in school that day. I don't remember what it was that upset me, but I will never forget what he told me that evening. He asked me to look up at the sky.

The stars were starting to come out. As happens sometimes, both the sun and moon were visible. There was a chill in the air. When he asked me to look up, I reflexively asked, "Why?" He patiently said, "Paul, just look up."

I asked him what I was looking for. Aren't we so focused sometimes on finding some needle in some haystack? That's what I was doing then. My dad smiled and said, "Up there, you will see space, room with no walls, no doorways, no exit ramps, no stop lights, nothing. And if you just remember to look up, you may one day understand everything. You will see sky. You will see nothing, but the open space. You will see everything there is to see if you let go of limits and witness the limitless."

160

He continued, "The sky goes on forever. There is no beginning. There is no ending. It just keeps on going." He also told me that we can't usually comprehend this because we are so used to limitations. To boxes. To walls. To barricades. To barriers. To doors to walk in or out of. To windows to open and close.

The concept of closed, off-limits places affects us. We start to limit ourselves. But if we are part of the limitless, why can't we, too, be limit free? There is a world . . . our planet . . . sitting in the sky and on all sides of it the sky just goes on forever. Decide to connect with that part of you that is part of the sky or part of the mountain. That little moment with my dad shifted my thinking about my place here and gave me the conviction that I must constantly seek out the larger story to be told. Making a choice to live large and as part of something greater can silence the wolf.

Ever wonder how some people make it look so easy while others always seem to struggle? Why some are filled with energy and others drain the energy of those around them? In *The Celestine Prophecy,* the narrator explains that some people are energy suckers, exhausting to be around, while other people give us a boost. The difference between being an energy sucker and an energy booster ourselves is having a connection with something more than our daily chores, based on the understanding that we have the ability to connect with the universal story.

The feeling of there being a universal story was reinforced at Esalen during a week I spent with a wonderful teacher and practitioner of instrument-assisted meditation named Anna Wise. Anna has written a number of books, including *The High-Performance Mind* and *Awakening the Mind.* On this retreat, we delved into brain waves and received real-time feedback. Anna taught me how the four brainwaves—beta, alpha, theta, and delta— "talk" to each other and pass knowledge from the conscious mind to the subconscious mind and back again.

Beta waves are associated with our typical waking activities. Alpha waves are associated with daydreaming and light meditation. They are a bridge of sorts to the theta and delta waves. Theta is the creative wave pattern. Many believe it is associated with extrasensory perception. Delta waves are present during deep sleep.

All the brainwave experiences I had that week were mind opening, but the delta meditation we did connected me to the memory of the evening I spent looking up at the sky with my dad. Anna told us that delta consciousness is the gateway to the universal mind. Is it possible that we can access all knowledge? Can we literally connect with the limitless? Can the knowledge and information of all humanity be accessed through delta brainwaves? If so, how can that be done? Can everyone access the information? Those were some of the questions we explored.

We engaged in meditation and visualization. We journeyed to the far depths of our minds to retrieve answers to questions we didn't consciously know the answers to, and yet answers were retrieved. Anna was wonderful to work with. She opened doors on how to see and feel things differently. She taught me to go deeper into myself to find a path to get out of my own way in order to uncover universal truths. When I left her program, I knew there was more.

The decision of spirit is about whether or not we choose to tap in to the whole. Each day we can be part of something bigger than us. Each day the universe is within our reach. Knowledge, art, adventure, and the passion of the universal mind are within our grasp. If that is so, then the decision of spirit seems to have the potential to mean everything. If the alpha is the bridge and the delta is the source of universal information, what does that say about our potential to be a person living outside of time constraints and age constraints?

We take comfort in the beta wave state. But the typical waking, active, thinking, solving of daily problems beta mind is so narrow. We might figure we can think our way through every problem or challenge. We might rack our brain searching for the answer. Then we discover the answer is there, but not only in beta. Beta is just one of four possible minds we can use. If we could harness the four, what worlds would open for us? Creativity and problem solving at a whole new level, an extrasensory capacity? Does this provide a portal into the intangible, invisible world that holds the secret for the meaning of this whole journey? Could we train ourselves to enter the sleep cycle alert and bring back the answers that we all seem to crave? Is the history of the world available to each of us if only we choose to cross that bridge?

In my week with Anna Wise at Esalen, we worked on the balance of these four brainwaves. Our goal was to be able to flow between them. It was exhilarating to me that I could decide to tap in to a world of possibilities. Some people find a similar experience in a religion. Some find it in nature. Some find it while playing extreme sports. We can find it anywhere so long as we get out of our own ways. This is how we bring into our world the potential of the whole world. The intangible and tangible worlds await an awakened spirit. This is accessible to us all.

If for some reason my story of brainwaves does not resonate for you, look at the pictures taken from the Hubbell Space Telescope of galaxies that are millions of light years away. We have not seen beyond those wonders yet. What is out there? How high is high? How awesome does the universe have to be before we will stop fretting about a perceived slight in an exchange with a friend or a bad day at work?

163

Let go and see the miracle that you are right here, right now.

The wolf only howls in the small, closed spaces of the mind. It does not howl in the stars and in the outer borders of the universal mind.

Decision #4: Learning

We can keep learning and growing. We can make the decision to be excited about finding something new to study. I see too many individuals reach a point where they stop growing. Then they begin to vegetate. My wife is not one of them. One of the many qualities Margie embodies that amazes me is her desire to continue learning and experiencing new things. She is committed to finding new challenges. I don't necessarily mean formal education, although she has received both a master's degree and a doctorate in social work. She has worked as an adjunct professor and started a nonprofit organization with a friend to counsel survivors of childhood sexual abuse. I mean she wants to learn new things because it is joyful and keeps her young at heart. From learning sign language to being trained as a yoga instructor, knitting the coolest sweaters and scarfs, weaving, studying feng shui, and cooking the best Turkish meals, Margie is always learning. She is the constantly engaged in the art of living life to its full potential.

After we married, Margie dropped out of college. Then, after giving birth to our two great daughters, she went back to school. When the girls needed guidance in school, she studied every program, school, and opportunity to make certain that they found their own unique paths to success. Her attention paid off. Each of our grown daughters is a dynamic, bold, and successful individual in her own right. Both are a blessing to those around them and their families.

164

When Margie finds something interesting, it consumes her. She fills the house with books, articles, class agendas, and more. She loves life. This is the joy of realizing the potential of a single day. Her joy in every day rubs off on me. Once something gains my interest it calls for all-out study. It could be something mundane, such as finding out who makes the best leather jackets for motorcycle riders, and understanding why they are the best, or something sublime, such as how to implement the Four Agreements written about by Don Miguel Ruiz in his book of the same name.

Sometimes I think people in our culture have lost sight of quality in their relentless pursuit to acquire more stuff. Quality is part of the invisible, intangible world that doesn't get the coverage it so rightly deserves. We seem to reward crass and loud things more than quiet, subtle things, such as beauty of a ray of sunlight as it hits the side of the mountain at just the right angle. Only by growing, studying, learning, and keeping our eyes wide open to possibilities does the day stay alive and vibrant. In this way, the mind is too active and filled with potential to become the tool of the wolf in the wee hours of the morning.

Have you made the decision to keep growing, to learn? I once heard someone say that learning doesn't matter since we all die eventually anyway. True, no one gets out of life alive. But that shouldn't be confused with living the life you've been gifted with to its fullest twenty-four hours a day every day, no matter your age or ability. Learning will stretch you and keep you vital. Whether by taking classes at a local community college, studying a new language at home, or going to a lecture series alone or with company, remember that your life is one massive ongoing classroom. If life were just one day—and in the grand scheme of things, it is—then why would you waste it on stagnation?

165

The hue and cry is that we can't find the time. There is that old excuse again. Time is the only thing that we have which, if not used, can never be used. Why not be wise with it then?

If your life was a college class, what would the textbook look like? Or what would be the title of the course? *The Salvation of . . . ? The Fall and Rise of . . . ? The Ten Lessons Learned from the Life of . . . ? The Meaning of a Day Seen Through the Eyes of . . . ?*

How does the syllabus read? What lessons are there in the study of your life? What will the midterm and final exam cover? Do you think it would be a popular class, one in which students could learn how to live their lives better?

Where does education fit? What part of us constantly wants to know more? Nourish it.

Decision #5: Fun

Upon returning home from the Himalayas, I made the decision to enjoy life and not take myself so seriously. By enjoying life, I do not just mean playing games, though games can be fun; I mean appreciating the day. I mean enjoying myself even in the most challenging of times, finding passion inside me so I don't have to keep searching for passion someplace else.

Considering that the Earth has been here for billions of years, have you ever stopped to think, relatively speaking, about how short a moment we are here? Our lives are a fraction of a day in the grand scheme of things. The only time we've got in the eternity of time is today. Our slice of eternity is now. So how are we eating this precious slice of the eternity pie? Are we worrying over the crumbs with the wolf or savoring every morsel of it? Balance must be found between the serious and the playful in life. The point is that fun must be a part of the life equation.

Let's move back to our consideration of the day. There was a time when I always thought the party was someplace else. Wherever I was, even if I was at a grand party, I thought the better party was down the road, around the corner, in the next room, or being held on another night. Then one day I saw a picture of a young woman in a small village in Ireland. She couldn't have been older than twenty. She was walking alone down a dirt road and looked so content, so present in the moment. The story under the picture was something about the simple farming life in her small village. At the time, I wondered how she could be happy there, as the village had no fancy restaurants, new movies, live shows, or nightclubs. Then, it hit me. Wherever she was, that was where her party was.

That old Zen Buddhist phrase again: Wherever you go, there you are. That picture helped me see that either I could bring the passion for my life with me wherever I was, even if I was home alone on a Saturday night, or I could keep going from place to place, job to job, relationship to relationship, spouse to spouse, looking for someone else to fill the passion void in me.

What decision have you made to live a life of passion, fun, and adventure? You are charged with creating your own joyful day. Whether at work or home, or in any other setting, don't let events or the behavior of others sap your desire to live your one day fully and happily.

As to toys and games, they are an important part of the single day. I have met too many people who frown on play because they do not think that it is a worthwhile way to spend a day. Their usual comment is, "When will you grow up?" As if adults aren't supposed to have fun! Has your life gotten so complex and serious that you miss out on being a rascal sometimes?

Try emulating a child. Kids live in the moment. Their play opens a world of imagination and adventure, of risk and the testing of their skills. Fun could help you let go and be present. You should try it more often.

For me, playing is riding motorcycles. There's something about them I enjoy. They are basic. Sleek. Dangerous. Open. It's also the noise. Being in the fresh air. Not feeling boxed in. Having no distractions. I love the whole ritual of riding, a step-by-step process where the ordinary is left behind and the possibility of discovering something new about myself still exists. From the boots and the leather jacket I don, to the gloves, sunglasses, and helmet, dressing to ride is a Zen-like experience, which I find fun. My routine existence is transformed through respecting the importance of each movement, of each zipper being adjusted to make the jacket or gloves fit just right. Each part of the ritual is vital to a safe and fun ride.

Isn't that the case with any joyful experience? It is not only the activity, but the process leading up to it, the slow build up to the rush of the actual game or sport that heightens our energy. This is when the initial rush of adrenaline kicks in for me.

Then there is the bike herself. I have saddled up on sport bikes, cruisers, off-roaders, and hotrods. Each has its own feel and story. Each can take me to the same place a different way. Over time I have learned to appreciate the little things about riding: the feel of the gears shifting, the smell of the open road, a biker wave from a passing rider.

Years ago, reading Robert Persig's classic book *Zen and the Art of Motorcycle Maintenance,* I just knew that sooner or later I would ride a motorcycle through different parts of the country pondering what this

168

journey through life is really all about. To some extent, this book is my stab at writing *Zen and the Art of Finding the Meaning in a Single Day.* That to me is fun. I love to ride and ponder questions like:

- How do I measure time?
- How do I measure the quality of a day?
- Where does kindness come from?
- Where does empathy for the plight of others reside?
- Why can't people just give each other a break?
- Why can't we give ourselves a break when we fall short?
- What has value/true worth?
- What will I remember at the end of this crazy ride?
- What does a caring person look like?
- Can I tell my kids I will always be with them, even as I let go?
- Would I give the ultimate sacrifice for the ones I love?
- Can I stand by my word even if it means I come in dead last?
- How much will I push to be all I can be?
- Can I speak truth to power?
- Can I simply lighten up and not take it all so damn seriously?
- Can I love with abandon?
- Will I finally stop listening to the critics?
- Will I trust my inner voice?
- Can I find peace even in the most disruptive times?
- Can I go gently through the day?
- Will I make it easy to be my friend?
- Will I finally appreciate how fragile and frail this all is, and treat life and the single day with the loving attention it deserves?
- Can I stop trying so hard to be right?
- Can I relax into being wrong when I am?
- When I fail can I fail with style and class?

- When I win, can I win with humility and gratitude?
- Since we are not promised any part of life, can I be present for that which I have in any given moment?
- Can I break a bad pattern?
- Can I embrace the honest effort?
- It is not possible to truly understand how we have found ourselves in the exact place we find ourselves at any moment, so can I accept the fact that I will never untwine the differently colored threads that have made up the fabric of my life?
- And, since the randomness in life must be accepted, and the fabric cannot be unraveled, can I then accept where I am and be present to it?

These are just some of the thoughts that race through my mind as I ride the streets, back roads, mountain ranges, and sandy coast lines of America. The motorcycle gives me the time and space simply to be, and that can be pure pleasure.

I have never understood those who believe that life is about work and play is reserved for children. If we are blessed, our work can be total enjoyment. But do not forget that in and of themselves play and fun have value and so are an important part of any day.

We must make time to play. Maybe for you this will be something entirely different than riding a motorcycle or participating in a sport. But whether your form of play is golf, tennis, chess, jogging, bicycling, walking, swimming, sculpting, writing, or dancing, find it. It doesn't matter what it is so long as you introduce yourself to the child who lives inside the adult you. The inner

child is looking to be released. The child has never left. He/she may have been silenced, but should no longer be. Make a decision to set the child free.

Within each of the five decisions a path to a full day exists. Within these five decisions, the texture of a life can be woven together. We must sit down and have a serious conversation with ourselves. The gift is too precious to throw away. But make no mistake about it, without choices being made in these categories, the hollow cave inside us is very likely to fill up with a pack of demon wolves that is searching for a lair in which to nest and multiply.

Health, family and friends, spirit, learning, and fun are the keys to experience the value of a day. When we finally take the plunge and appreciate the day for the opportunity it provides to expand us, we are investing in the asset that is us. Each day apparently stands alone, but there is really only one day. So begin now. The midnight mind can rest if it knows we have made clear decisions.

CHAPTER 20

The Hole Inside the Hole

We sat around on a warm Florida evening a few years ago. There had to be fifty or more friends who had come together to celebrate a life. The life we were toasting was of a beautiful, vibrant, smart, close friend, someone involved in the life of her family who was living the last few weeks of a life that was coming to a very painful end much too young. We had witnessed her bravely struggling with the devastation of amyotrophic lateral sclerosis (ALS), also known as Lou Gehrig's disease. It had completely taken its toll on her. Her muscles had become weaker and smaller. The motor neurons in her brain and spinal cord were damaged. Movement was lost. Then Cindy became a prisoner in her body. It is an insidious disease. She could still see, hear, smell, and feel. But it had stripped away so much of the essence of being engaged in the fullness of the day. For Cindy, it made each moment seem more vital.

As in all things, the ending was part of the story. The circle of her life was slowly collapsing in on itself. The mix of songs being played covered every musical taste. There were Peter, Paul and Mary, Bob Dylan, The Kingston Trio, and Judy Collins tunes, with a few from Leonard Cohen thrown in. Leonard Cohen's songs "Bird on a Wire" and "The Traitor" have always haunted me, and they did so on this night. To me those two songs are all about trying our best to be free even when the odds are not in our favor—while remembering that no matter how hard we try there will be some "judge" criticizing even an honest effort. We may fail, and the odds are that more times than not we will fail, but even so trying to be all we can be is a beautiful aspect of human nature. It is in the striving to be where our identity lies. In the reaching, the simply being. We each must keep trying in our own unique ways to be present in the day. We each must resist letting the critics pull us down. The critics have nothing better to do. It is their job to frown and look for imperfections. But we must keep on reminding ourselves that it is the imperfection that makes us who we are. I heard it said that we are all perfectly cracked cups. It is fine to simply be as we are flaws and all. So long as our intentions are honorable, the naysayers can naysay all day long.

Both of the songs weave tales of an effort being made. They inform us that although we may never break away from the fears and negative influence of those who are trying to bind us and hold us back, we must keep trying to move forward, no matter how strong the head wind blows against us. Never forget that life is lived in the efforts we make.

On this night, as the songs were being sung our friend was taking it in. She had a glow to her face, expressing her knowingness.

She knew that each second was precious and one of the last of a finite number of seconds. She realized that each touch was probably the last time she

174

would touch those who mattered to her. She looked around with such a peaceful look on her face, a look of finally understanding. She understood what it meant for this to be the last contact, as far as any of us knew. As I wandered from friend to friend, gradually making my way toward Cindy, I felt a hush come over the group. Finally, I sat next to her. I took her hand in mine and we just looked at each other. It felt like she was studying my face, as if she knew that she somehow would be able to recall it on some other plane. Her skin was paper thin. Her mouth was dry.

She could make a few words work. It was difficult, but not impossible to communicate, if you leaned in and went to a place where communication was more than just words. Our communication was from the heart and there was an understanding between us that transcended words. She, in her way, then quietly said, "Paul, will we meet again on the other side."

I told her, "I hope so." I commented that I had to believe friendships and love last throughout time and we carry our friendship and love with us.

She then said something that penetrated my very core. She stared up from her physical prison and falteringly whispered, "It was so easy being your friend." Each word was caught by me.

Could there ever be a more beautiful compliment? Why do we sometimes test the ones we love? Why do we make it so hard so often just to be with someone whom we care about? My thoughts took me back to Mount Everest, the monastery, and the wholeness that I had felt there. I told my friend I felt the same way about her.

Easy. Light. Gentle. Kind. Sweet. Blissful. Engaged. Hopeful. Decent. Honest. Sincere. Noble. Content. These were the words triggered in me when I thought about her and our friendship.

Why is it that some make life so hard and difficult, especially the lives of those who matter most to them, while others make life soft and easy? She always made it easy.

Finally, it was as if a light shone down on her. She looked down, as if searching for the exact right words to say, but it was just too hard.

That night we celebrated a life. We and our companions laughed and cried. There was clarity in each connection. Not too long after that evening, she passed away.

I can recall a conversation Cindy and I had at an earlier time when she was a bit stronger, but still knew that her life was fading too fast. She sat with me and said: "I am ready to see what this next place looks like and I know it is time to let go of where I am. I want to be released. I am so tired. And I know I am a burden," (she was not), "but I am going to miss seeing how everyone's story plays out—what choices my friends make, what paths life holds in store for them. Will they figure it out before they have to let go? I am going to miss waking up next to my love. I am just going to miss drinking a fresh cup of coffee as the sun is rising. I remember school and being so worried about it all. How I looked. Will the boys like me? Will I have a date for the prom? All the fretting about things I would like to fret about now. I am going to miss you. I am just going to miss the single day and watching the sun break through the clouds."

When we attended Cindy's funeral service, her husband released butterflies into the sky. I watched as they fluttered through the air and vanished. She loved butterflies. She used to say that her soul would be carried to the other side on butterfly wings.

Every day you are born. Each day is a do-over if you choose it to be. Each morning can be a rebirth, if you choose to believe it is. You can never be too old to appreciate the day.

How does your story play out? How do you decide to live your day?

What direction will your kids take? Will they figure it out?

Can you start giving your friends and family a break from being perfect? Can you stop judging yourself and others harshly? Can you enjoy making the effort for the effort's sake only?

Each day is the quest. Each day is the endgame. Each day in and of itself is the prize. The day is the meaning. The day is the purpose. We choose how to fill it. Can we fill it with passion for what we have been granted?

A single day, the last one of its kind, is a rare commodity. Perhaps if days were traded on the New York Stock Exchange people would treat them with the same tender loving care they give to their hedge fund investments. Do you see the insanity of ignoring the meaning of the day?

Do you feel as if there is a hole inside you that you keep expecting someone else to fill up? Those holes can never be filled. It is a variation of the dichotomy paradox of the Greek philosopher, Zeno. The paradox is that if you fill the hole half way, and then , half of the remaining , and then half of what is left, ad infinitum, the hole can never be filled. There will always be an emptiness.

It's easy to become a slave waiting for someone else to fill the emptiness. Or are we waiting for a new car? A new relationship? A better golf club? The latest motorcycle? Whatever we are waiting for, once it is acquired it will be appreciated briefly, but the emptiness will return as soon as the newness fades. It is only from within that the hole can be filled. We can only fill it by telling our story, living our truth, and bringing our passion for the day to light.

For me, everything I do comes down to two

177

questions that must be answered.

- Am I telling my story?
- Am I being truthful with myself? Or am I telling myself a lie that I desperately want to believe is true but I must finally admit is a lie. A choice must be made. The waiting must end. The decision is upon me.

When I am nearing the end of this crazy thrill park ride that is life, will I regret that I never told my story my way? By "telling my story" I mean, made my own choices and did what I wanted. Will I be wondering what I was so worried about? Will I be proud of the legacy I left behind? Did I help? Was I present? Or was I one of the shadow people, one of the pretend people, one of the awake dead people? Will I be just be some outwardly expressed form of my own wolf? The wolf is the part of me that knows when I am cheating myself out of my life.

A good life is one in which we are telling our tale each and every day. Our way. With our voice. We must be authentic. Nobody else knows what is going on inside us. So we cannot merely follow another's lead. It won't fit us. The worst that could happen from being our genuine selves is that we will fail. But if we are authentic, at least we can know we tried. Since the great equalizer waits for us all, we must try in our own ways to be genuine.

When I tell people to make certain they are living a life that is consistent with their truth, by making their own special journey based on what matters to them, I often get looks and comments such as, "What are you mumbling about? I am just trying to get to Friday night and get drunk (or hook up with someone)." People like that don't understand my powerful desire to make the most of being alive. Each day. For me, each day is the first and last day.

178

Thinking about the end of my life and what it means to value the day makes me think about Peggy Lee's song "Is That All There Is?" I was too young when I first heard the song to fully appreciate its meaning. But as the years went by, I understood that haunting song better and better. If, on my last breath, I were to say "that's it?" then why didn't I just let go and dance?

Couldn't we each let go and dance our own special dance? That's all there is.

The second question I ask myself frequently is what lie have I been telling myself that I want to believe is a truth? Something I must now admit is a lie.

Haven't we all lied to ourselves in one way or another on different occasions? Have we wanted to believe a relationship was working when we just knew everyone was miserable? We refused to risk a change and just kept telling ourselves that it will be fine when we know it is not? Sooner or later we must admit the one lie that we can no longer live with. It must be confronted so that the day is truly ours to live.

I sat with a dear friend recently and asked her these two questions. The first one was comfortable for her to answer. When we got to the second one, she broke down in tears. As she sobbed, I asked her what was going on inside her. She wiped her tears away and said, "I need to come to terms with the fact that I am just not needed in the way I need to be needed." She realized that it is about her insecurity and nothing else. She said that if she could accept that truth she could let go and move on. She did let go. She did move on. She finally let that lie die.

We can manipulate everyone into believing some tall tale, but once we look in the mirror we know what we see. We must drop the mask—just let it fall to the ground. We must accept ourselves, imperfections

179

and all, and embrace our truths.

How do the five major decisions discussed in the last chapter relate to the two questions? They are intertwined with the choices we make. What lie do we know we can no longer live with that pertains to our health, to our family and friends, to our spirit, to learning, to simple enjoyment? Are we telling our story so that the choices we make are consistent and in unity with what we want to stand for? Have we become so weighed down with falsehoods that we can't lift ourselves up any longer?

So we are coming full circle back to the hour of the wolf. The witching hour. The midnight mind. For the wolf lives in the hole inside the hole, the hole that only we can rid ourselves of by making choices about the things that matter to us and speaking our truth with integrity and nobility. We can silence the wolf by living life's journey in a way we can be proud of.

In the search for the meaning of a single day I have traveled to different countries and experienced different cultures. I have ventured into the inner depths of my soul. This inner space exploration was challenging. Wherever I went, I ventured into the recesses of my being. My travels have taken me to the Himalayas. I have crossed the ice fields of Mont Blanc. I have bicycled through the French Alps, hiked the Matterhorn, and paraglided off a cliff in Chamonix. Each experience challenged me. I have studied with shamans and energy healers. I have learned about the high performance mind and explored the potentials of the four brainwaves. I journeyed to the other side in visualizations to retrieve my power animal and learn lessons from my parents and friends who have passed over. I have had doctors perform the

most intricate of surgeries on me and freed myself from pain and the drugs that were supposed to deal with the pain. I have sat with friends who have gracefully let go. Their dignity in the face of the unknown was inspiring beyond my feeble ability to even fully appreciate it all. I have witnessed people saving themselves from disaster and others being consumed by disaster. Always, I ask, "What is the value of a single day?"

My search has taught me that the single day is all there is. A life is but a single day in length. Our Grover's Corner is here. So we must appreciate it all, whether we are falling or getting back up on our feet again. We can choose to live in fear, implicitly inviting the wolf into our lives or we can live with courage, and have faith in the improbable journey we are on and relish it for all it has to offer. The choice is in our individual hands.

I have come to agree with Larry from *The Razor's Edge*. The road to salvation is narrow and as sharp as a razor's edge, but we must walk it. There is no way out. We must seek the meaning to our life. What do we stand for? What does our life mean? What is our purpose for being here?

Find what brings joy to you and your family. Identify what exactly brings you bliss. Too many lives are out of balance. It feels as if the pinball machine of life is always blinking on tilt. Everyone seems to be trying so hard. So yes, you must find the balance.

As you reach corners that you must turn, seek out the wise and associate with the gentle. Sit with the elders and learn their secrets. Keep striving for the possible. Choose with courage and risk the impossible.

It was at the monastery where I began the journey to find the meaning of my life. I have since realized that how I live my life each day is the meaning of my life. For this life is never to be repeated. I understand that I have no option but to live my life as boldly as I can. I want to live with love in my heart. I want to experiment with growing older with grace and style.

The various gates I have passed through have been transformative. The gates have helped me realize that limitations are self-imposed. Whether physically challenged or not, reject any signs that say you can't do what you want to try. I intend to try until the very last breath, and only then to let go. That is my ageless experiment.

CHAPTER 21

The Ageless Experiment

As we sat around the dining room table, we four good friends talked about the latest news, the Hollywood tabloid gossip, the recent movies we'd seen, and how good the dinner had turned out. There is nothing like old friends. We can just be who we are with them. We know each other's successes and failures, highs and lows, our children's misadventures, and have reached the point in life where we can laugh about it.

Margie and I had just come back from a trip to Turkey where we celebrated her sixty-fifth birthday. Wandering Turkey opened up a whole new world of ideas and adventures. From Istanbul to Cappadocia, Bodrum, and Fethiye, we had thoroughly enjoyed this diverse, ancient, yet modern country. There was something about immersing ourselves in a culture that has been around for so long and visiting a land that has survived so many different societies and conflicts that helped us put our life in perspective. Maybe that is why we kept the conversation going as we reentered the United States.

183

After having seen so many "lost" civilizations and contemplating how they lived and died, I couldn't help thinking about my place in this process.

At this point, my friend Bruce asked, "So where do we go when we die?" This wasn't said in any morbid way, only as a continuation of the other topics of our discussion.

After some nervous laughter and a few one-liners, Margie responded, "We're just gone. I guess we go back to where we came from."

Although we know that this world will continue after we are gone, we can make a positive difference in the lives of those we love, both while we are here and even after we are gone. We pray that we leave a positive legacy. We want our kids not only to remember us, but also to better understand and confront the challenges they will face, by the lesson that is our life.

Most of us don't like to think about the end, but it is the reality. The trick in a life is to become one with this reality, to come to terms with this truth. Once we address this unforgiving fact, we can lighten up and see the value of the single day for what it is. My chance to genuinely enjoy my day is born from this knowledge.

Death seems sometimes to be a massive sleight-of-hand trick. A magic show where we are the one who disappears. Margie's answer seems as right as any answer I've heard. We return from where we came. But where exactly is that? Are we pure energy? Are we here but in a different form? Just maybe this explains my meetings with my parents during my Esalen retreats.

If we continue, then, what are limitations about? What are restrictions and boundaries about? Couldn't we live outside of any barrier, self-imposed or not ? What is the reason not to?

184

My sister is a world champion worrier. That

is just her nature. She almost takes pride in being a blue-ribbon worrier. Her breathing is always shallow since she forgot how to relax and breathe a long time ago. As we were catching up with each other at a family gathering, I commented that if she worried a little bit more, she would pass the some benchmark of worry and live forever. She gave me one of those " I'm annoyed by you" sister stares, then started laughing.

I told her, "Look, you're going to die whether or not you worry, so let go of the worry. Experiment with breathing. Experiment with laughing. Experiment with enjoying life for just what it is in that moment."

Once you let go of worry and the fear of death, aging becomes a farce, timelines of events take on an absurd texture. What matters is whether we live our lives by our own definition of who we want to be each day.

I know that to some readers this may sound so obvious. It may sound almost like an innocent's chatter. But please just stop for a minute and meditate on this simple truth, because it is an undeniable truth: We only have the day—and even that isn't promised to us.

I recently attended a business meeting with a group whom Tom Wolfe refers to as the "masters of the universe" in his wonderful book, *The Bonfire of the Vanities*. You know the types, the self-appointed business movers and shakers. As I wandered around the room popping in on different conversations, I picked up on a theme. The talk was about money to be earned, new cars to buy, latest gadget to possess. Then I heard one woman say that she wished she was twenty years younger and knew what she knows now. She wanted the wisdom of the years lived with the energy and physical youth of an earlier time.

That comment stopped me. There was sadness

185

in her tone. I thought, *What just happened to the wisdom acquired over all these years?* It seemed to add up to nothing much if the wish was to just go back. I chimed in, "But you are here today and know what you know now. Use that wisdom now. What would you do differently? And why not start today?"

The response was that she was too old. She said she couldn't do the things she wanted to do any longer. There was not enough time left.

My view is that there never is enough time. And the time that we do have seems to be wasted on thinking about how it could be spent in a time that no longer exists. That's a lie the woman really needed to admit to herself. To me, it seemed she had bought into the whole aging fallacy. The fallacy that a day has less meaning simply because someone has lived longer than someone else. Somehow, she'd bought into the crazy illusion that the day lost its power due to us being a year older. When I remarked on this, she looked at me as if I had sprouted horns on my head. Her cry was, "I can't. I just don't have the time. I don't have the strength."

How many times have we heard or even said that excuse ourselves? I have come to believe that it is this single thought that catalyzes the aging process more than anything else. It is this one false premise that blocks us from taking the path to being all we can be today.

In truth, the day does not discriminate. Only we discriminate during the day.

I love being outside and taking in nature in her various forms and moods. Nature just is. The rain cleanses. The sunrise inspires. The sunset is as close to a religious experience as there can be. It is timeless and ageless. We embody those things, too. Because we are part of nature our very existence should be inspiring, our being should be recognized as the religious experience that it is. Our tears cleanse us. We are a mini-universe. We will take on different forms as we get older. We will see another wrinkle here and there, or a gray strand of hair, but this is just nature in her dance of life. We must join that dance every day. We must be engaged every moment.

I reject the limitations society tries to impose on me as I age. I started writing my blog, "The Ageless Experiment," to reinforce my rejection of society's false assumptions, especially the idea that somehow there is less meaning in the single day because of an arbitrary date on the calendar. I truly don't get it. I also don't want my children and grandchildren ever to feel as if time is the enemy of their adventures. Time is merely the medium through which we navigate as we experiment and experience life. Time has no agenda. Time doesn't come with instructions. It is simply there for us to do with what we will.

After reading Mitch Albom's book *The Five People You Meet in Heaven,* I sat down and wrote a letter to my kids and then put it away. I put it in a spot where they could it find fairly easily as they go through my papers once I am gone. What I wrote was: "Kids, if you, by some chance, find this paper, and if by some chance unfold it and read it, I want you to know about ten people that changed my life for the better whom you may have never met, probably don't know, and may have never heard of, yet your life is better because they helped me when I needed help and shone a light for me when I lost my way."

I then wrote about ten people. Some of them I only met for a moment, yet they inspired me to be more and work to overcome an obstacle. They taught me to laugh in the face of danger, and wisely choose the exit strategy. I wrote about those people who left their imprint on me and my family. One such person gave me my first big break. Another helped me up when I had failed miserably and believed I could not get back up. One just made a passing comment to me that affected how I treated everyone else I met from that moment on.

That man, a revered and highly successful businessman and banker, told me that he always stopped to learn the name of everyone he met, no matter their station in life, and thank them for the big or small service they had performed that made his journey easier. It didn't matter if it was a cab driver, an office cleaner, or a waiter in a luncheonette. He wanted to appreciate them all. That one comment taught me to be grateful. Now I never take simple kindness for granted. Kindness is ageless.

I concluded my letter by saying, "Be grateful for the subtle gestures. Learn to see the gifts that are presented to you in all the different wrappers they come in. And then be one of the ten to another in their journey. Live a life where there is a clear moral legacy left for your family."

My blog has become my moral legacy for my family and friends. Do you have a similar moral legacy to leave to your loved ones? Something that expresses what you believe, what you would stand up for, that for which you would drop everything?

Don't be a mystery to those in your life who matter. Don't leave your children wondering what you really believed. Don't be afraid to share your fears and dreams with them. Help your children understand they are not anomalies by letting them know that you, too, worry, dream, and have the same concerns as them. We all worry and dream about the same things, but no one talks about them. They need to feel safe in their uncertain moments. They need to see that you kept going no matter the discriminating barriers put up against their progress, like sexism, racism, ageism, or some other

"-ism." An "ism" should not define them.

Can we experiment with living beyond "-isms" and expectations? Can we experiment with pushing ourselves to new heights, whether it is twenty years later than before? Can we challenge ourselves to let go of what is no longer working for us and seize the possibility of what we can still be?

I started riding motorcycles when I turned fifty-four. I saw no reason not to. It is challenging. It is a dangerous sport. It is so much fun. Only someone who rides a motorcycle understands why dogs like to stick their head out of car windows at high speeds: It just feels liberating.

I decided that I would do CrossFit when I turned sixty-four.

I have not changed. Society might feel more comfortable if I were to "act my age," but I don't really know what that means. My ritual is to get up each day and try to fill it with another adventure, and this is unconnected with time and clocks. I'd encourage anyone to try the same thing.

The meaning of a single day knows no boundaries. Don't impose limits on it.

In the end, my search for the meaning of a single day led me to the undeniable conclusion that I am as Mount Everest and Mont Blanc are: ageless. I am simply me today, and the day always holds a promise of unlimited possibilities if I believe it does. The ageless experiment trumps the howling wolf at midnight that is the fear of limitation, and dying with adventures untried.

I pray that you release yourself from the grip of fear of failure at any age. I pray that you release yourself from any self-imposed limitations. Keep challenging yourself. Never forget that you can begin your next adventure at any spot along this road we call life. It is not over until you say it is.

189

RESOURCES

Contact Paul by Email
Theagelessexperiment@gmail.com

Connect with Paul via the Social Networks
Facebook.com/TheAgelessExperiment
Twitter.com/PaulRLipton
LinkedIn.com/PaulRLipton

Subscribe to Paul's Blog
TheAgelessExperiment.com

Hire Paul to Speak at Your Event
If you're looking to mix things up a bit and create an experience people won't be able to stop talking about, look no further. Paul Lipton is an experienced speaker with a charismatic, yet down-to-earth presence who will inspire, motivate, and connect with participants in ways very few can. His stories leave people laughing out loud one minute and on the edge of their seats the next.

He shares, without holding anything back, and he leaves his audiences with actionable ideas that serve them both in their work and lives. Paul inspires audiences to become agents of success to themselves and those around them.

Recommended Books

A Collection of Essays by George Orwell. Mariner Books, 1970.

Awakening the Mind: A Guide to Harnessing the Power of Your Brainwaves by Anna Wise. J.P. Tarcher, 2002.

The Bonfire of the Vanities by Tom Wolfe. Farrar Straus Giroux, 1987.

Encyclopedia Britannica's Guide to Normandy 1944 (see "Mulberry")

The Five People You Meet in Heaven by Mitch Albom. Hyperion, 2003.

The Four Agreements: A Practical Guide to Personal Freedom by Don Miguel Ruiz. Amber-Allen, 2001.

Futility or, the Wreck of the Titan by Morgan Robertson. 1898.

A Hermit in the Himalayas by Paul Brunton. 1937.

The High-Performance Mind by Anna Wise. J.P. Tarcher, 1997.

Our Town by Thornton Wilder. 1939.

The Razor's Edge by W. Somerset Maugham. 1944.

The Snow Leopard by Peter Matthiessen. The Viking Press, 1978.

Tao Te Ching.

The Tibetan Book of the Dead.

The Upanishads.

Way of the Peaceful Warrior: A Book that Changes Lives by Dan Millman. HJ Kramer/New World Library, 1980.

Working in a Very Small Space: The Making of a Neurosurgeon by Mark Shelton. Vintage, 1990.

Zen and the Art of Motorcycle Maintenance: An Inquiry into Values by Robert Pirsig. William Morrow, 1974.

Recommended Videos

180 Degrees South: Conquerors of the Useless directed by Chris Malloy. 2010.

The Big Chill directed by Lawrence Kasdan. 1983.

Brigadoon directed by Vicente Minnelli. 1954.

Dust to Glory directed by Dana Brown. 2005.

The Ghost Army directed by Rick Beyer, 2013.

The Great Escape directed by John Sturges. 1963.

The Longest Day directed by Andre Marton, Bernhard Wicki, Darryl F. Zanuck, and Ken Annakin. 2006.

Saving Private Ryan directed by Stephen Spielberg. 1998.

The Spanish Prisoner directed by David Mamet. 1998.

Star Wars directed by George Lucas. 1977.

ACKNOWLEDGMENTS

I would like to acknowledge:

My mom and dad, Lorraine and Maurice Lipton, for teaching me to lighten up even in the darkest hours. Although they both died too soon, their teachings live on forever.

My sister, Heather Seidel, for always being there as we figured out our way after our parents' deaths.

My dear friends Steve Lederer and Cindy Silverman, who showed such dignity during their last illnesses and untimely deaths.

My editor, Stephanie Gunning, and her partners, Stephany Evans and Peter Rubie, and the rest of the fine team of professionals at Lincoln Square Books, including Gus Yoo, who did a wonderful cover and interior design. They shaped and clarified my story in a way I never could have imagined.

To all my friends who kept telling me to "write that book, Paul." Thank you for your persistence.

I am grateful to Rabbi Irwin Kula, Nan Moss, David Corbin, Stephen Gibb, Barry Richard, Scott L. Rogers, Arthur J. England, and Craig Borders.

To my two amazing, beautiful daughters, Melissa Jones and Lindsay Gerszt, who teach me every day what it means to be strong, decent, loving, and caring. Thank you for your constant support.

To my two sons-in-law, Mason Jones and Brad Gerszt, thank you for joining our family and being part of this journey.

To my three incredible grandchildren, Ryan Jones, Reghan Jones, and Hunter Gerszt, who are wise beyond their years and bring light, humor, and wisdom to my day each day. They teach me the meaning of appreciating each day on its own terms.

None of this would have been possible without Margie. I am so blessed to have Margie in my life. She is the most genuine person I have ever met. She has given me unconditional love and support in all I have attempted and accomplished. This book is my ode to my wife.

Thank you all.

ABOUT THE AUTHOR

Paul R. Lipton is an attorney, a speaker, a legal consultant, and a blogger. He is currently a co-chair of the Eleventh Circuit Committee on Professionalism in Miami-Dade County, Florida. *Hour of the Wolf* is his first book.

As an attorney, Paul tried cases for more than forty years. He has litigated numerous jury and non-jury trials in complex commercial, probate, estate, and trust cases involving national and international companies. Paul began his career as an assistant district attorney in Nassau County, New York, before moving to Florida. Once there, he practiced law in a number of firms. For thirteen years, he was a trial attorney with the international law firm of Greenberg Traurig. Paul was a principal shareholder there at the time he retired from the active practice of law.

Paul is a frequent speaker to various bar associations, bank and trust companies, and law firm meetings. The topics he addresses in his speeches include finding a balanced life in a profession and world that seems out of balance, how to maintain professional conduct in an increasingly unprofessional world, and finding your moral compass in the uncharted territory of demands being made just to get the result no matter the consequences.

As an undergraduate, Paul attended Penn State University, where he was a member of the history, political science, and social science honor societies. He also performed in a number of theater productions, including *Brigadoon*. Paul then attended Washington University School of Law, where he was a note editor for the *Urban Law Annual*.

In 2010, Paul started writing "The Ageless Experiment," a blog on living outside limitations, with posts on finding the sweet spot in life where as you age you continue to challenge yourself to be all you can be without regard to age or any other definition, and without restrictions, either self-imposed or societally imposed.

Paul has been married to Margie since 1968. They have two beautiful daughters, Melissa and Lindsay, and two sons-in-law, Mason and Brad. Paul and Margie also have three wonderful grandchildren, Ryan, Reghan, and Hunter.

A longtime resident of Miami, Florida, Paul now lives in Boulder, Colorado.

29193001R00117

Made in the USA
Lexington, KY
16 January 2014